TRAGIC
BLESSINGS

Karen Solise

A MEMOIR

Blessed Beyond Ministries
Madisonville, Kentucky

Blessings!
Karen
12-29-22

DEDICATION

*W*hen asked to whom I would dedicate my book, I knew quickly that the answer to that would be my family. I am so very blessed when it comes to having supporting and loving people in my life. My extended family, my friends, my parents, my boys—I couldn't have done this without them. However, if I were to choose just one person, there is no doubt of the ONE: my husband, Preston.

Preston supported me early in our marriage when I spent endless hours pursuing my dream career of becoming a teacher. He endured the multitude of hours that I devoted to my students and instruction, and then he supported me multiple times as I continued my education to advance in my career field. He has always encouraged me, in ventures too numerous to name.

Preston not only encouraged and supported me when I shared with him that God had called me to begin Blessed Beyond Ministries. (God spoke that into existence when He said audibly to me that I am "blessed beyond measure." That is an entirely separate story for an entirely different book.) Preston also jumped in and became part of this ministry that God is continuing to grow.

Preston had a vision of me writing this book for quite some time before I did. He encouraged and supported me throughout this process but has, most importantly, believed in me. He waited patiently as God revealed His timing when He showed me that same vision. There are endless instances that I could mention, but I will merely summarize my thoughts with this: I am BLESSED. God's goodness, grace, and mercy are beyond my comprehension. I dedicate all that I am to Christ. I dedicate this writing to my husband, Preston.

*A*ntsy? No, antsy doesn't describe it. Uncomfortable? No, that's not it. Squirmy? Maybe. Unsettled? Now, that's probably it. I really just can't come up with the best term to describe my spirit in my early twenties. There is no one word that sums up my spiritual state during those years. But I can tell you in detail what I was experiencing—as if it were earlier this morning that I had been feeling the feelings. And even though I'm not a betting person, I'll bet you've had the same type of experience at some point in your life.

To give you some background …

I grew up on a farm in a very, very, very small town in Kentucky. (Did I mention that my hometown is small?) My parents were your typical working-class parents. Dad was a machinist, and Mom worked in the local high school cafeteria. There was only my brother Jeff and me, so I made every move I possibly could to follow in my older sibling's footsteps. There were a couple of guys that lived near us who were friends with my brother and, since I was already a tomboy, I hung out right with that crew. Wherever the guys went, I went. Whatever the guys did, I did—to the best of my ability, anyway.

Recently, as I was traveling to Lexington to see my baby boy (a senior in college), I looked at the woods along the parkway and saw the streams flowing so peacefully from the melting snow. I could not stop myself from smiling as I reminisced about how I had spent my winters sledding down the HUGE hill of pasture in the back of my friend and neighbor Kirk's house. In the depths of the snow, we would fly as quickly as possible down the monstrous slope, only to slowly climb our way back to the top just to zoom to the bottom once more. My smile grew even larger as I recalled how my brother and I had enjoyed so many carefree days of exploring the woods and the land at my parents' home, slathering in the mud of creek banks and ditches; there was always an adventure.

Even though the guys thought I was the silly little girl, I always followed behind them through the brush and the thorns as each quest unfolded in the summer heat. They, of course, saw me as a nuisance; they thought I was just a tag-along and that I couldn't keep up. But I have a confession to make: The reason I was always sure to be in the back position of our pack was so that the boys would be the first to see any snakes or creatures that might be wandering around, and so they would be the first to come upon the briars and branches as well. Sure, the guys weren't happy that I was following them. But they were at least nice enough to clear the way for me. AND, for the record, as the sun beamed down and the guys went ahead, their height and placement always acted as cover for me. They thought I couldn't keep up, like I said. But really, all along, I was smarter than they gave me credit for. I was simply using them as my protectors. HA! Silly boys.

They tolerated me as best they could. They had to—I didn't give up easily. I guess it didn't hurt that my parents always made Jeff include me and "be nice about it."

My parents were just that: my parents. They didn't try to be my friend. They didn't maneuver to always make things go my way. They were my parents. They had rules they expected my brother and me to follow, and if we chose not to follow them there were consequences. But there was something I didn't realize—something I didn't figure out until I hit the "real world" in my adult life, my early twenties: My parents also bore the brunt of the world for me so that I could be a kid. I had no worries while I was playing in the creek. I wasn't concerned about bills or living arrangements while I was riding my motorcycle in the woods or sledding down that huge hill. My parents kept adult matters and concerns and hurts and pains and hardships to themselves. They fulfilled their role, enabling me to fulfill mine. The magnitude of their efforts and work was never quite apparent. Nor, as a beneficiary of their efforts and work, was I quite grateful for it all until my childhood was becoming a vision in my rearview mirror. As my twenties came into view ahead of me, I began to see and hear and feel the pain of people facing battles. It was all so completely out of my realm of experience, and it caused a heaviness to set in on me that I would not easily shake.

See, here's how it goes. I don't know when it started or what prompted it, but at some point in my early twenties, after I had married my high school sweetheart and given birth to two beautifully perfect baby boys and reached my goal of becoming a teacher, my sunshiny skies became clouded with my own shade of gray—my personally selected shade of dim gray. As I slid into mature, responsible adulthood, the realization of how blessed I was began to hover over me—like the steam hovers over the pavement in Texas in mid-July—and truly set in. In my transition from carefree teen to adult, I was beginning to see the world outside of myself and, quite honestly, it wasn't something I was ready for. The heavy weight of guilt became attached to me, making me feel like an octopus with all tentacles handcuffed; it was confining, and the keys to free me were nowhere in sight. Guilt about the blessings in my life became the norm. There was incomprehensible suffering on every edge of my being, yet the goodness that surrounded me continued to prevail—creating in me seemingly insurmountable guilt.

Crazy, I know. Irrational? Yes. Again, I was in my early twenties, and I hadn't been off the farm much. Give me a break.

The ability to savor simple daily pleasures—like a walk with my babies or relaxing with the sunshine on my face—was beyond me. Guilt consumed me to the point that I did not enjoy the ease and stillness of my life. I had no idea how to be still and how to be thankful for the calmness, contentment, and peace. Accepting my life as it was and praising God for His blessings, yet recognizing the harshness of the world and praying for Christ's hands in the situations around me—I just couldn't handle the paradox. There was no separation of circumstance. I felt the need to take on the pain of others through guilt. It was as if I REQUESTED turmoil or turbulence, like I wasn't really being an adult if I wasn't personally experiencing painful encounters. It was beyond my maturity level, and my mental and spiritual grasp, to intellectually understand (which I could) the concept that God wants to bless His children and give us the desires of our hearts, yet emotionally deal with the reality of that truth (which I could not).

Little did I know that it would be years before I would begin to see the truth that Christ wants to give His children—sons and daughters, heirs to His Kingdom, you and I—fullness of life. Even now, I can't say that I fully comprehend this truth. It is my belief that I will not completely grasp the fullness of God's love until I meet with Him face to face, walk with Him, and talk with Him. God wants to teach us as His children, and at this point in my life I was forcing him to teach me. I was calling his hand.

No wonder my life was about to get really full.

*E*ver heard the expression, "Be careful what you pray for"? Well, never has there been a more true statement. In the blink of an eye, and as quickly as the heaviness of guilt had become an appendage to me, the bottom fell out of my picture-perfect world—and the appendage was amputated for lack of relevance. I no longer saw reasons in my life to feel guilty that things were so smooth and easy for me. As a matter of fact, I began to feel very little; my energy was too focused on surviving life's struggles and disappointments.

Take your pick as to which event would offer the service of ending the guilt I had carried for so long. Was it the experience of three miscarriages when I wanted so badly to have a baby, and the heartbreak I suffered with each loss?

Was it having a son who had severe food allergies (which no doctor was aware of for a newborn back in 1989) … and who experienced numerous health issues and hospitalizations beginning as early as six weeks old … and who didn't form any sleep patterns, staying awake nearly around the clock until he was three and a half years old? YES, three and a half! Little Clay would cry and scream in pain continuously, leaving both my husband Preston and me exhausted and perplexed. It took us years to pinpoint our son's illness as food and environmental allergies.

When we did finally get a diagnosis, it seemed to bring on a whole new realm of issues. Because these newly identified allergies did not constitute your typical, average ailment, many people—including family—were very skeptical and were hard pressed to believe that it was vital for our son to avoid certain foods, ingredients, environments, and allergy triggers. Since I was the mom, I caught most of the backlash and criticism. Many people made it clear that they felt I was simply being overprotective, while others implied that the idea of "allergies" causing such extremes in a child was ridiculous and definitely inaccurate—so they didn't take our requests seriously. Either way, Preston and I knew how our child was suffering and how we were the ones living in the situation and doing so while dealing with little to no sleep. Preston, being the night owl of the family, would stay up with Clay each night until one a.m., at which time I, being the morning glory, would begin my shift of childcare. It was hard for us to attend family functions or even simply be out in public. Avoiding allergy triggers became a lifestyle—a lifestyle that left us secluded in many ways, due to others' perceptions that we were being too extreme and dramatic. Being the mom, I saw it as my job to protect my son no matter what the expense of the loss I suffered. But that constant focus on protection quickly drained my being and placed me in a mental zone resembling the preparation for combat. Guilt was no longer in my vocabulary. I was now programmed to defend and protect.

What else could have pounded my guilt into a cloud of dust? There is no shortage of possibilities. Was it the four surgeries I had undergone to deal with a medical issue I had faced? Was it the accident I'd had that had done an enormous amount of damage—but not quite enough to total the vehicle—just two weeks after purchasing a car that for nearly six years I had admired and planned to buy for myself as a graduation gift? Was it the issues I was having with my kidneys not working properly for, according to doctors, no apparent reason—issues that had a tremendous negative effect on my health? Was it the time when my younger son, Tanner, at age five, contracted a potentially fatal virus, ended up in the hospital for nearly a week, had a fever of 106 for a few days, hallucinated to the point he didn't even recognize me, and nearly died?

Maybe it was when Tanner started experiencing severe asthma attacks. On multiple occasions I carried him into the emergency room of our local medical center because he wasn't breathing. During one such event, he had stopped breathing when we were still a couple of minutes out from the hospital; by the time I packed him in my arms and rushed him through the double-entry doors, his color was gray.

There's that color again: gray. At the risk of overusing the word (or the color), I have to go with it—because it truly is the best descriptor. Gray is so telling and so symbolic of numerous aspects of my life at that time. You see, gray portrays a sense of mid-hue: It's not white that speaks of brightness and life, nor is it black that indicates closure and death. Gray reflects limbo, neither alive nor dead. That was my state of heart, mind, soul, and spirit. And to be honest, the discoloration of my life was the result of choices I had made. One choice after another creates our life path, and my choices had directed mine.

I didn't need to feel guilty about being too blessed anymore because I couldn't find a glimmer of peace or stability or calmness anywhere. My life as I had known it was crumbling; my peace had fallen to pieces. Eventually, I had no hope. But God knows our hearts. God knows what we need. He works all things to the good of those who love Him. Believe it. God knew my choices didn't necessarily reflect my true heart, and He loved me enough to not leave me where I was or allow me to continue in the direction I was headed.

All of these events happened within just a few years' time. Tanner's asthma attacks were especially scary and exhausting. On average, he was in the ER or at the doctor's office three to four times a week, every week, for the duration of these years. It became a vicious cycle of medicines, improvement, and downslides.

If you're familiar with asthma at all, you probably know that it's like many sicknesses in that it worsens at night. That was most certainly true for us, which meant I was often home by myself to deal with it—since Preston worked the third shift. Whenever Tanner had an attack while Preston was at work, I'd have to call my mom to come and stay with Clay in our home. Even on those comparatively rare occasions when Preston wasn't working (and could therefore stay home to take care of Clay during one of Tanner's attacks), I'd end up being the one to take Tanner to the hospital—by myself, alone. That word—*alone*—holds so, so much significance. There are times when "alone" represents solitude, while at other times "alone" connotes dark-ness and emptiness. There is a tremendous difference between alone and lonely. For me, at that time in my life, "alone" surely represented the dark and empty loneliness.

So it may go without saying, but I want to be very clear: Just as my sweet Clay could never sleep because he was sick from food allergies (not to mention his own struggles with asthma), there was very little sleep for my precious Tanner either, due to the severity of his asthma. All of which meant that sleep deprivation was the norm for me for about ten years after I had children. The anxiety I experienced was almost paralyzing. Each day was a kaleidoscope of overpowering emotions. I always felt such intense pressure. Pressure watching Tanner play ABA (American Basketball Association) basketball, and wondering if this would be the day he collapsed or stopped breathing. Pressure monitoring Tanner's myriad medicines. Throw in a few other toxic emotions on top of it all: I was angry about having to be the one who juggled all these balls, and I was envious of those who (apparently) didn't have to endure the never-ending heaviness that pressed down upon me.

Most of the people in my life were probably clueless about the intensity of my days and the war I fought within. I never reached out for help because I felt that in doing so I would surely confirm my weakness and my failure as a mom. The one thing we did do—in an attempt to save time and money, not to mention improve our sleep—was finally purchase a nebulizer machine. It went everywhere we went, including school. I took it to my school each day so that I could go over to Tanner's school during both my morning and afternoon planning periods to give him his treatments. The routine, though convenient since God had given me a teaching position in the middle school next door to my boy's elementary school, was overwhelming and exhausting. Anger, bitterness, fear, envy, loneliness, resentment, and feelings of drowning began to overtake me. I had gone from continually feeling guilty because of the abundant blessings in my life to feeling as if I was in a barrel screaming at the top of my lungs and absolutely no one could, or cared to, hear me. Working full time, coaching the dance team at the school where I taught, operating a household, being a mom—keeping up the pace was taking its toll.

Not only did I feel jilted because I had to carry the load of what felt like two or three people; I also felt robbed in my role as a mother. I had been forced to take on the role of caregiver/nurse on a round-the-clock basis, and I missed being able to view things from a mother's perspective. As time progressed, the wall of bitterness became taller and taller, thicker and thicker. Looking back, I can see that I missed the opportunity to nurture my boys the way I feel a mother should—with a healthy combination of risk and development—because I was continually protecting them and acting from a place of fear. What's even more saddening is that I overlooked the nurturing aspect of parenting not only for Tanner but also for Clay. Because Clay was so quiet and therefore so rarely in the foreground, he required—and received—little attention.

Recognizing all of this was sickening for me, causing only more anger. The overwhelming sensation that pieces of me were literally crumbling and falling from my body had definitely taken the place of the guilt. The more Preston worked, the more I felt like I was carrying the weight of the family. And over time, that lie became truth to me. My mind became fixated on believing that Preston was providing only financially, and that I was providing financially AND doing everything else. I know this isn't pretty, but it's honest. It's how I felt. Breathing in and out was more than I thought I could do most days. All the while I was maintaining a career, a household, and a family—or at least what was left of one, given that I was driving an hour and a half from my home at least one night each week to take classes toward a master's degree, to say nothing of coaching and going to all of my boys' activities. To be completely honest and brutally transparent, in my skewed perspective and limited vision of my life and for my life, it never dawned on me to remove some responsibilities from my plate. I was so busy and overwhelmed that I could not think clearly. There is a magnitude of truth in the statement, "If Satan can't get to us and destroy us, he will distract us enough for us to destroy ourselves." That was definitely the case for me.

I never did a self-audit, a cost analysis, a life inventory. COME ON! I was an undergraduate business major, and I'm a business educator. I should have known to examine each thing I was investing myself in and analyze the return on that investment. But I was so caught up in the "do" cycle that the costs I was paying and the costs attached to my choices eluded me. It never occurred to me to just stop, reflect, and make changes. I was too busy to stop! Satan didn't have to expend much energy on me because I was indeed destroying myself. Understand this. I wasn't destroying myself because I was so busy, but because of the way I handled my "busyness." My busyness was controlling me, consuming me, taking me over. I had no time or room in my life for love, relationships, joy, peace, or blessings. Every fiber of my being was wearing thin. I was the Stretch Armstrong toy of the 1980s. Stretch was a popular toy/"doll" made of rubbery material that allowed him to stretch. He was quite flexible, and you could pull the parts of his body and stretch the material to amazing lengths. The problem was that the more you stretched him, the less resilient he was. The more his body was pulled in different directions, the more disproportioned he became. And as he became more disproportioned, he became more useless. Stretch Armstrong: That was me. Except I felt like "Stretch Arms Gone" because I couldn't handle one more thing. Numbness was my desired state, but my reality was far from it.

On top of, or because of, the chaos of sick kids, job demands, class work, and all the rest, my marriage of fifteen years was at its lowest, thinnest, weakest point—from my perspective, at least. You may not see the significance of the phrase "from my perspective," but it truly is important for me to include it. Why? Because Preston, to this day, is steadfast in saying that he wasn't in tune to anything being wrong. Get this; it's important. While I felt as though our relationship, our marriage, was destitute and nearly beyond repair, Preston thought our state of being was just how marriage and life were supposed to be. Was either of us unhappy? No. But were we truly living life? NO. We were co-existing, believing that's all life would bring. Did we have two perceptions of the same relationship? YES, and those perceptions fell at totally opposite ends of the spectrum. We were surviving, not thriving.

We were both longing for so much more from our lives together. While I was desperate for emotional rest from carrying the weight of worry about both of our sons' sicknesses—not to mention mental rest from juggling the ten million things I had on my plate—Preston was dying for physical rest from working sixty-five-plus hours a week as a coal miner, coaching our boys in one or more sports each season, and attending every activity our boys participated in. (Preston's company worked him sixty-five-plus hours every week; this was not optional. I will be brutal here in saying that IF WE LET IT, our job will take the place of our family. What successful business owner would encourage you to not make him/her more money?) Individually, we were suffering and yearning. But as a couple we were making no attempts to change or improve our status. Preston was doing what he thought he was supposed to be doing, and suffering in silence. I was doing what I thought I was supposed to be doing, and suffering in silence. The problem was that we were doing what we thought we were supposed to be doing according to a worldly perspective, not a godly one. We didn't know the godly perspective. We knew God, but we had no idea what it meant to have God as our Lord and the leader of our every action and decision.

Now, what's crazy is that I can't pinpoint one certain thing that serves as evidence that my marriage was at its weakest. Nothing was really wrong, yet it was all wrong. The more I felt overwhelmed, alone, and lonely, the more my mind convinced me that Preston wasn't pulling his weight and that I had to carry my family. The more exhausted Preston became, the more his mind convinced him that his role as a man was to just work as hard as he possibly could push himself, even if it meant his life was to just be an existence. I bought into the "you should be taking care of me and making me happy" mindset, while he bought into the "I have to work as much as my company needs me and provide my family with everything they could want to prove myself as a man" mindset. I was relying on Preston to make me happy, and he was relying on his job to prove his manhood.

I have fought the battle of having low self-esteem and an all-consuming lack of self-worth since I was very young. For some reason, one that I have yet to uncover, these feelings intensified to a new level when I was about seven and became more of a controlling, life-directing issue for me. As my life unfolded and I dealt with the many circumstances that came my way, my feelings of inadequacy and low self-worth skewed my vision and heightened my thoughts of disarray in my marriage and life. The feelings I had about myself made me focus on the struggles life was throwing at me, which only bolstered my feelings of failure. In fact, I put that label on myself with an adhesive that had the strength of an elephant. I was self-proclaimed and self-diagnosed as a failure because my life was less than perfect, out of control, and not going as I had dreamed it would go.

The world had Preston and me right where it wanted us. Actually, let's just call it as it was: Satan had us right where he wanted us. He wanted to tear apart the love we'd had for one another since high school. We were co-conspirators in many ways. Instead of talking about things and bringing issues to the light, we each sealed our lips and drifted deeper within ourselves. It is a daily, conscious decision to seek to live as God has planned and not as the world dictates. There is more wisdom than I can express in the scripture that the truth shall set you free. God is our only hope, and we must rely on Him! Satan wanted to see our family dissolve into vapor, and we were falling for his tactics. We were not connecting. Our surface was rough, and our edges weren't fitting. As a couple, we didn't even realize our connection was slipping away from us. I think we both saw that a barrier was building between us, but neither of us initiated talking about it. We simply didn't have the time or the energy. Our lives were full—full of noise. Deep, dark, black, heavy noise, the kind of noise that causes people to lower their heads and trudge forward as if they are walking against the pressing wind of a winter blizzard, the force of tornadic rotation, or the whipping rush of waves in a hurricane.

Preston and I traveled this road for as long as we could until we came to an ominous "no outlet" sign, which in turn led to an abrupt, steep cliff. Our problems had become harder to avoid than to simply acknowledge and accept. We had subconsciously gone along with things as they were and had ridden the roller coaster of ups and downs, being thrown from side to side between acceptance and denial, acceptance and denial—until that ride derailed. We eventually got to the point where we weren't silent anymore. We would bicker about anything and everything. It was continual jabs at each other, disagreements about the simplest of things, like the toothpaste tube. But that's how we expressed our discontent with our relationship and the hand life was dealing us—we bickered. I can honestly say that we didn't fight. We didn't have anything to truly fight about. But this is where we get blinded. Our humanness just accepts things. We accept mediocre; we accept survival and existence when we were made for so much more than that! Preston and I weren't unhappy. We just weren't living in abundance and joy.

I've never wanted to be one who just lives; I've always wanted to thrive. But the state of our marriage was just the opposite. There were snarls and huffs and eye rolling and smirks and tones. Oh, the tones. And we were so mature about it, too. Preston would say something and I would come back with a rebuttal or some slur to let him know that I was bothered by his mere speaking. I would do something that would compel him to give his look of displeasure—the one that implied I had done whatever IT was, and that let me know he had a better way. Both of us became adept at belittling the other in such snide ways that other people might not have caught on if they hadn't been on their A game.

Preston and I actually expended energy to ridicule and oppress each other at every opportunity. It was hardly surprising, then, that we sank deeper into our worn-out ways—mentally, physically, and spiritually. If we had just stopped and asked ourselves if the issue of the moment was even worth being an issue, we might have saved ourselves a great deal of wasted breath, energy, turmoil, and hurt. When we talk about it now, we can't help but laugh and wonder how our kids survived the tension. Our behavior was so very unfair to our boys. Preston and I were like two kids on the playground, arguing and saying, "My daddy is stronger than your daddy." It's quite embarrassing to acknowledge and admit that. Thank you, Heavenly Father, for the fact that it is all quite comical to us now.

To be fair, even in the midst of all the turmoil and emotions, we both knew that, under the surface of the mess, we loved each other deeply and we couldn't bear the thought of being without one another. Simply put, seeing it from this side, we were just using one another as targets, as mutual catch-alls, because we were each the person the other felt closest to. You know the saying that the ones we hurt the most are the ones we love the most? We proved that statement to be true, over and over again. Do you have someone in your life who fills this role? Someone you're close to who feels the brunt of your anger? Is there an undeserving target of your hurts, disappointments, stresses, fears, and maybe even self-inflicted issues or wounds? Maybe you don't necessarily speak harshly to this person. But are you placing blame on him that he doesn't deserve? Are you dealing with her in anger because of other things you cannot control in your life? Are you ignoring him, intentionally or unintentionally? There may be someone in your life who is not getting the attention or recognition she deserves because other things are monopolizing your time and energy. This person may be your biggest supporter, sitting quietly as you give everything you have to the things that demand your attention.

Either way, whether this person is your target as a catch-all or your target as someone to neglect, now is a great time to talk openly with him/her. You may mend some fences that you weren't aware were broken.

I'm just thankful that this particular season of our lives was oh so brief where Preston and I were concerned. Whew.

As harsh as the battles were, and as tumultuous as that time in my life was, somehow in the midst of the chaotic storm, as we reached the eye of the hurricane, God showed me His never-ending mercy and granted grace. He spoke to me.

3

*A*t the time, I wasn't sure what the heck was going on. But as Christ began to chip away the anger, peel back the bitterness, tear down the walls of resentment, and develop in me buoyancy in my state of drowning, things became more and more clear.

Ever had a nagging feeling that something just isn't right, or that you're missing something? "Did I turn off the oven?" "Did I let the dog back into the house before I left?" "OMG, did I pay the water bill?" You know, things that make you question yourself, that you simply cannot shake, that just plain nag at you? Well, sometime in late fall or early winter of 2003, dealing with persistent, nagging feelings became as much a part of my daily routine as brushing my teeth—and as invasive as flossing them. Every day, out of nowhere, the sense that something just wasn't quite right would come over me. Sometimes it would attack instantly, while at other times it would creep in rather slowly and I would be pondering on it before I realized what was happening.

This went on for months. I initially brushed it off as just being a part of my crazy, chaotic life, schedule, and responsibilities. I thought the tension was simply the result of the juggling act I was trying to maintain while walking a tightrope. It seemed like someone had signed me on as the main attraction in the circus and had neglected to tell me!

The feelings became so persistent that I began sharing them with one of my closest friends—you know, one of those friends you can say anything to, even if you sound like someone from another planet, and they won't get all freaked out or just blatantly laugh in your face. That kind of friend. After months of having this weird feeling hovering over me, I finally broke down and told Libby that my gut was telling me something big was coming; something was going to happen. Libby's response, just as I expected, was to listen intently, wonder about the possibilities along with me, and reassure me that she knew I wasn't crazy and that things would work out. We had this conversation on more than one occasion. I even went so far as to share with Libby my suspicion that these nudgings had something to do with Preston.

I want to reiterate that anger, bitterness, and resentment had replaced what were once feelings of guilt about all the blessings that had surrounded me in my life. But let me be clear and specific here. While most of my emotions were aimed at my husband, he had no idea how I was feeling about and toward him. In all the turmoil that life was throwing our way, we both did what we thought we were supposed to do. I took care of the kids, the house, the activities, the bills, the schedules, and the health issues. Preston worked eighty to ninety hours a week. I thought I was supposed to be able to do everything. My view was that, as a woman, my role was to manage all the tasks that revolved around the house, the household, and the kids because Preston was working and didn't need to be bothered. Preston, meanwhile, worked as many hours as his body would allow because he thought his role was to provide financially, never miss a day of work, ensure we had good health insurance, and be present and attentive to our boys. Neither one of us had the right idea! We had never taken the time to talk about what our roles would be or should be. There wasn't time! We just silently fell into step with what each of us perceived to be our own roles according to what the world was showing us. Neither of us was overly thrilled with the way this whole "life" thing was going. But God. God was in control. God gave us strength. God kept our marriage together. God did not let us have our own way. I see now that God truly had a plan and was working in our lives all the while.

Even though my feelings toward Preston were far from loving and nurturing, God began to impress upon me—in the midst of all the uneasy, "something is going to happen" sensations— the importance of praying for him. So I began to catch myself praying for Preston regularly and intently. I would go to the walking track in our town to walk and talk to God. I made it a priority to find this time for myself and pray for Preston. I would pray for his safety, pray for a hedge of protection over him, pray that I would love him more, pray that our love would be renewed, and pray that I would see him as God saw him. Seeing people as God sees them brings us a whole new level of freedom. It's not that God sees perfection; He knows we aren't perfect. But He sees beyond our flaws and our scars. He looks at all of us as He created us to be. He sees purpose and our potential, whereas we stop looking at the first sight of a blemish.

I didn't really like Preston at the time. Trust me, I know how horrible this sounds. I wish it weren't so. But I think it's really important that I be completely honest with every aspect of our story. Divorce was starting to be entertained, in my head at least. It never went past being considered for a brief moment. But it had indeed crossed my mind that it might be easier for Preston and me to divorce. It was yet another of Satan's lies that I was tempted to buy into. The idea of having one less person to care for was enticing—for a brief moment, as I said. But when I stopped and thought of the reality that divorce would mean I would no longer have Preston in my life, what had once appeared enticing turned quickly to repulsive. Apparently I was just going to continue being so bitter toward him that I couldn't think straight. Yet I couldn't fathom the thought of being without him.

I don't know what I was thinking.

Truth be told, we didn't know each other at this point in our lives. Our relationship was suffering. Our family and our home were suffering. Please hear me on this. Too many times, we, all of us, try to hide the imperfections of our lives. We don't want others to know that we have struggles because we feel it would show our weaknesses. Too many times, we try to hide behind a smile and a simple "I'm fine. How are you?" Let's be real: We all have struggles. We have imperfect marriages, imperfect children, imperfect homes, imperfect lives. And maybe you, like me, have been at a point from which you thought there was no return. But God. God is greater than all of our imperfections and has all power and authority over our lives.

I would vocalize my thoughts and feelings as I walked at the small park near our home. God already knew how I felt, so I decided I might as well be open, honest, and real. I told Christ that I had no idea what was going on or what was to come, but that I wanted to genuinely love Preston and that I wanted God to protect him. For months, I experienced an internal battle—as if an intense archery practice was going on within me. Deep, out-of-nowhere, quick punches to my gut became regular pains I had to deal with. My intuition constantly warned me that something was coming. It was all so relentless that I once again shared my thoughts and suspicions with my friend Libby. She always listened and never judged or laughed. As I look back, it may have been the ability to voice my concerns to Libby that made me even more committed to prayer. Hearing myself express aloud that I felt something was going to happen to my husband—well, that may have been the very thing that acted as a defibrillator for my heart and put it back into the right rhythm. Talking about things has always been one of my ways of coping. Sharing is therapy for me. Perhaps that's why, to my surprise, the sense of dread and heaviness I had been experiencing would eventually turn into a dutiful, yet peaceful release—along with audible, clear voices.

*P*reston had worked in the coal mines for most of our marriage, which meant swing shifts and odd schedules. It was VERY rare for us to go anywhere or do anything as a couple. Heck, with his work schedule and our boys' own busy schedules, it was rare if we had ANY time as a couple. If we ever did happen to be at the same place at the same time, it was at a ballgame or church, and typically we didn't arrive or leave together. We came from different directions and left heading for different places. Talk about two ships passing in the night; I'm not sure we were in the same ocean.

As we began to see the true state of our relationship, we decided we wanted to do something for ourselves as a couple, something that would help keep us an "us." And here's where I'm going to disclose one more layer to our story. I know. How much more can there be, right? See what I mean by chaos? It's a web, but it was our life. At the time, Preston and I were also experiencing changes in our church attendance. We had been worshiping in a church body that I had grown up with. We loved the people. We felt God's presence meet us there. And we loved the heart the people there had for serving others for Christ. Our worship time there had seemed to be the one constant in our lives; it was the one place where we were content.

But Clay had recently attended a youth group gathering at a different church nearby, and he began asking us to visit the church and consider going there. There were very few young people in the church we were already attending, and Clay had several friends who were a part of the youth group at the new place. So in the interest of trying to do everything we could for our family, Preston and I decided to attend the new church for a few Sundays, talk with our boys about it, and, most of all, pray to seek guidance about this big decision.

We enjoyed the new church, but we loved our own as well. We just weren't sure that changing was the right thing to do. On the other hand, we knew it was crucial for our boys to be involved in a church body so that they would, at their ages, stay plugged in. So in mid-March 2004, we began attending the church Clay had requested and worshiping with a new body of believers. Ultimately, this decision would illustrate once again how God is in control of every single detail of our lives. It ended up serving as evidence to support the wisdom of Romans 8:28: "And we know that in all things God works for the good of those who love Him, who have been called according to His purpose." Even though we weren't living our lives for Christ, He was working all things together for our good—and had been since the moment we had accepted him as our Savior. God doesn't operate like a video game, waiting for us to live up to His standards, complete a checklist, or perform at an optimum level before rewarding us with a prize. Instead, He instantly rewards us as a new living creature the moment we ask Him into our hearts and accept Him as Savior.

Here's the part of this story that blows my mind: Even though we felt guilty about basically attending two different churches at the same time (we'd only done it for two full weeks, but we felt as though we were cheating on our original church), God was completely okay with us doing so. As a matter of fact, God encouraged it. He knew that both bodies of believers had people within them whom we would need in the time to come. And He made sure to have our paths cross with those of others who would feed into our lives exactly what we needed to deal with the present, face our future, and make the changes necessary in our own little world. God placed people around my boys who would envelop them during the trials to come. The boys would need these people, and God provided them at just the right time. God worked out that detail. We weren't cheating on anyone. We were actually following the whispers of God as He orchestrated His blessings into place.

Even though we hadn't attended services at our original church for two weeks, we'd heard that it was beginning to offer *The Purpose Driven Life* book study on Sunday evenings. We felt that, even though we might have to leave early from some of the meetings, we would at least be doing something together. It would be a committed one hour each week that we would set aside just for us.

When I felt the yearning to ask Preston to take the class with me, I had absolutely no clue this study would be a spiritual marker that would impact my life even to this very day. It turned out to be one of the most impactful decisions I'd made in my life to that point. As I began reading the book, the words immediately reached to the core of my being. And after years of living with Band-Aids on numerous wounds and trying to hide the hurt and the pain by masking the scars, I finally experienced the depths of me coming to the light. I felt myself being raw, revealed, and real. Everything was coming to the surface. All of the inner darkness was being pierced by the light of truth—real truth, truth I couldn't run from. Paralyzing truth.

The class began on a Sunday evening. We met as a group, got the material we needed, went through an overview of how we would spend our time, and received our first reading assignment. It was the beginning of my spring break from school—something teachers and students alike live for—and I was PUMPED. I was thrilled that Preston and I were going to do this study together, that we would actually have one hour each week to be together and with adults, that we would have something other than responsibilities to talk about. I had never been so excited to read anything. Never had studying God's word brought out such excitement in me. Saying this brings shame to me now. But at that time I was merely a Christian. My walk with Christ had dwindled to a crawl, at best, and my only hope was that I had accepted salvation.

Two days later, on Tuesday, I was sitting on the steps of my front porch. The flowers smelled as strong as cinnamon rolls right out of the oven, and the fresh-cut grass with its sweet aroma made me think I was back home on the farm, playing outside and rolling in the yard as a young girl. I remember feeling the warmth of the sunshine as I sat with my eyes closed and simply soaked in the smells and the sounds of the lake water, the horses, the birds, the breeze, and the trees around me. There was no better place for me to dig in and complete my assigned reading for the day.

This would be another pivotal moment—a life-changing decision.

In *The Purpose Driven Life*, author Rick Warren states that we all have a purpose, something specific that we are created to do—something that, if we don't do, God will use others to fulfill. This concept hit me as if I had taken a blow to the gut in a professional wrestling match. I read this passage in the book over and over again. It couldn't be! I didn't want to miss what God had for me! I didn't want to miss doing what I was created to do! I couldn't fathom the thought of God using someone else to fulfill His mission because I was too consumed and off course by distractions. I did NOT want this to be my life! I did not want God to think He couldn't rely on me!

The more I read and reread the passage, the more I saw the depth and darkness of the lies I'd been believing and what those lies were taking from me. I finally began to spot the lies for exactly what they were.

One bald-faced lie that I had always accepted as truth was my deep-seated belief that my worth was equated to my performance. Yes, this was a lie from Satan that I had fallen for hook, line, and sinker. I felt as though God didn't love me if I didn't perform well and work for Him. I had put a worldly perspective on my relationship with God that if I messed up, He would be mad at me and would want to punish me. I envisioned God sitting in Heaven waiting for me to make a mistake or not live up to His expectations so that He could wash His hands of me or belittle me. I knew I didn't want God to be counting my failures and looking for reasons to leave me alone.

I was doing those things enough for myself, God, and everyone else. My performance ruled my mentality. No matter what I accomplished, it was never enough. I was never enough. I could go for days or sometimes weeks without the beast appearing. But when it did, it was all consuming.

Never had my internal belief made itself so apparent as when I read what Rick Warren shared through his writing: That God had a purpose for my life that only I could fulfill. It was as if the words were spoken directly to me. It was these words—even though I had read the Bible, accepted salvation, and knew from a young age that Jesus loves me—that penetrated my eardrums and my heart. I finally heard that God had created me for something specific, which meant that I had to have been made just like Christ wanted me. I figured out, at long last, that performance has nothing to do with God's love. Obedience is the key. Once that light penetrated my darkness, I knew that the most important thing in my life was to be obedient to God and His plan, not mine.

So then and there, right there on my porch, I literally told God out loud and clearly that if it was His will to take Preston, I would need the strength to take care of my boys. "God, if you need Preston, then I understand, and I will rely on You. But please, God, remember that we need him too. I need him. God, help me to accept what You have for us." After reaching that mindset and place—and after finally being completely honest with myself and Christ—I sat for a long while there on the porch steps, just listening. Listening for God. Listening to His creation. Listening to my heart.

The next day, Wednesday, my boys and I had spent the morning shopping when we decided to stop off to eat before heading back home for the night. As we were being seated, I experienced something I never had before (nor have I experienced it since). Someone said to me in my right ear: "It's just you and the boys now." I immediately turned to see who would say such a thing, but there was no one around. I questioned both boys about it, and they responded as though I had three heads. They insisted that they had said nothing to me. Maybe it was the waitress, I thought. So I questioned the boys again: Had the waitress been beside me and, if so, had she said something? Once again, the boys responded as if they were viewing life from another planet and weren't quite sure of the motives of the said alien.

No one had spoken these words to me. Yet I had heard them.

My first instinct was to grab my phone and call Preston. Had something happened? Was I losing my mind? My fingers couldn't dial fast enough for my racing heart. As soon as Preston picked up I felt a tidal wave of relief pour over me, something like what I experienced when I recently took part in the Lou Gehrig's Disease Ice Bucket Challenge. The feeling washed down my being from the top of my head to the soles of my feet. Preston's voice calmed me like I hadn't allowed it to do in such a long, long time. Our conversation, though brief, was pleasant and reminiscent of "us," the high school sweethearts, the Karen and Boo I had grown up knowing. There was a glimpse of us being right again.

It was 5:34 a.m. exactly when my eyes focused and I reached my hand out to stop the annoyingly loud, disruptive noise that had just awakened me from a deep sleep. When I saw what time it was, I completely anticipated a prank caller or a wrong number to be on the other end of the line. Never did it dawn on me that I would set in motion the beginning of a chapter of my life from which I would never return—a chapter that would change me in ways I could never have predicted. Picking up that phone would turn out to be answering a call from Christ that would change the course of my life, my children's lives, and, dare I say, the lives of my descendants for generations.

It's unbelievable how clear it all still is to me.

"Sissy"—that's what my dad has always called me, and it is one of the most endearing ways I have ever been addressed, alongside "Momma." My husband, meanwhile, has been called "Boo Boo" since he was a toddler. His family called him Boo Boo, and it stuck. Family, friends, teachers, even sports announcers and the local newspaper reporters called him Boo while covering his high school sports career. Anyway, I digress only to offer some essential background information—because the caller on the other end of the line wasn't a prankster or a misdialer. It was my father.

Dad: "Sissy, I need for you to get up. Boo has been in an accident."

Me: "Oh, he has. What happened?"

Dad: "Well, I don't know. They're taking him to Owensboro."

Me: "Owensboro? Why Owensboro?"

Dad: "I don't know. You need to get the boys up and get them ready. Me and Momma are coming to get you. We will be there in a few minutes."

Me: "Ok, bye."

I have no memory of my dad saying goodbye. Looking back, I'm not sure he could bring himself to push out any more words while he was simultaneously trying to push out the energy to keep himself together.

The calmness and peace I maintained throughout the call and while preparing to leave my home were, and still are, indescribable. It never dawned on me that Preston was hurt badly. I just remember wondering why in the world he or the mine staff would choose to go to Owensboro. (It was over an hour away, and we had a hospital twenty minutes away from our home.) Preston had been in minor accidents on the job before and had always gone to our local medical center. Heck, he had even driven himself there after his first incident in the mines. My dad had called me that morning too, about thirteen years prior, and I had been a wreck. After getting my little one settled, I had raced—yes, raced—to the ER, only to find that Preston had mashed the tissue out of the end of one of his fingers but had driven himself to the hospital to get his finger cleaned and sewn together. My bundle-of-nerves self had been aggravated at his "no big deal" attitude and approach. I had almost wanted to hurt him myself.

But this time—Saturday, April 10, 2004—the call, my reaction, the circumstances, the request to get my boys ready … it was all so very different.

After calmly going to the restroom, just as I would on a normal day, I headed upstairs to wake the boys. Clay was in eighth grade at the time, Tanner in fifth. The conversation was largely a repeat of the one I'd just had with my dad.

Me: "Clay, bub, I need for you to wake up. Dad has been in an accident."

Clay: "What happened?"

Me: "I don't know, bub."

Clay: "Is he okay?"

Me: "I just don't know. I need for you to get dressed. We're going to go to the hospital to check on Dad. Grannie and Granddaddy are coming to get us."

All the while, as we were having this conversation, Clay was waking up and getting out of bed, and I was still calm and matter of fact. It was so unlike me at that time. Years of chaos and disorder had left me very high strung to say the least.

After having almost the exact same conversation with Tanner, I turned to go back downstairs so I could finish getting myself together. I gave out one more call: "Now, you boys get ready. Grannie and Granddaddy are coming to get us, and they will be here any minute." It was in that moment that the rush of realization and heaviness began flooding over me. Ever since my oldest had been born, there had been numerous times when my mom had insisted she come to our house so that we wouldn't have to take my babies out of the comfort of their beds and/or home. Whether it be while I was taking classes or going to work—and whether it was in the freezing cold or the heat of summer, late at night or early in the morning—Grannie had always put herself and her needs behind the comfort and needs of my children. Why had Dad told me that we would be taking the boys with us? Suddenly the seriousness of the situation was becoming clearer. Yet the calmness I experienced—well, to this day I can only explain it as the presence of God.

Since Mom and Dad hadn't arrived yet and I was dressed and ready to go, I called Preston's brother Chad. I had contemplated waiting until I had more concrete information, especially because it was so early in the morning. But I knew that if it were my brother, I would want to be aware that something was going on. I didn't want to alarm Preston's mom or dad. His brother Troy typically didn't answer his phone. His sister, Panda, lived in Florida. And when it came to me deciding between Chad and Preston's oldest brother, Coy, Chad lived the closest and was the closest to Preston in age. Chad was a coal miner, too, so I knew he'd understand that I simply had no information at that time. So Chad it was.

I tried to make the call brief, telling Chad directly that the only thing I knew was that Preston had been in an accident and that he had been taken to Owensboro. Surprisingly, Chad's reaction was the same as mine had been: "Owensboro?"

As I was on the phone, my dad came in and the boys wandered downstairs. So I ended the call quickly with a promise that as soon as I had an update, I would call back and share the information.

Chad's response, tone, voice, and control were not calm and peaceful. Looking back, my demeanor may have seemed cold.

But I honestly believe that it was simply God's grace carrying me at the time.

As we climbed into the car and got everyone settled, the questions began to fly from my lips like swarms of bees in a hive. "Dad, how did you know about the accident?" This was the first question of many to come. "The mines and Denny called me," he responded. And we don't believe that God is in control, and that He orchestrates every aspect of our lives? Let me explain. This man, Denny, and my dad had been friends for years. Preston and I had become Denny's neighbors several years before the accident. And Denny, at that time, was working at the mines where Preston's accident occurred. The details of God's plan and design cannot be overlooked!

As we got onto the parkway and headed out on the hour-long journey, I—being the I've-got-to-know-what's-going-on person that I am—began to feel the need for answers.

"I just wish that I knew what's going on, what happened," I said. "Dad, tell me what was said and who called."

"Baby, it was Denny, and he just said that Preston had been in an accident and was hurt."

That was my dad's only response.

After trying to think of anyone and everyone who would have been working that night, I began to make a few calls. One person told me that an ambulance had been on scene when the rescue team got Preston out of the mines and to the surface, but that due to the extensive injuries and seriousness of the accident he had been put on life-flight.

After I told my dad what I had just learned, he called Denny again and finally got the details that made me fully aware of the fact that the *thing*—that pit-of-my-stomach aching that I had been praying for protection against—had indeed happened. We learned that Preston had been hit by a scoop pulling a pod duster. The only way people knew to describe it was that Preston had been run over by a piece of machinery. The man operating the equipment hadn't realized that Preston had been hit, and so he had continued to manipulate the movement of the equipment. Preston had been pinned against the rib, or coal wall, of the mines and had moved along the wall as the machinery had made a turn. His body had been folded in half and had contorted like a wad of paper.

When Dad repeated what he'd heard over the phone, paralyzing silence consumed the five of us for what seemed like hours but in reality was only a few minutes. As I processed all the information we had been getting, the flood of love and connectedness and need and belonging flowed over me like rushing water that pours forth as the gates of a dam are opened. The reality of "what the heck have I been doing?" began to soak in to my core. And yet the calmness and peace that had covered me from the beginning of this day continued to hold me.

When we were about halfway to the hospital, two counties over, I turned to the back of the vehicle and said: "This is the kind of dad you have, boys. This is the kind of dad you have. He's run over by a piece of equipment and has them call your granddaddy so as not to scare us or alarm us. He is hurt like this and is thinking of us." TRUTH—real truth, important truth, not a worldly perception—was becoming much more clear to me than ever before in my lifetime. I loved this man, I had always loved this man, and I planned to continue loving this man—even though I had told God I was okay if He needed Preston and I had relinquished my rights, as if God needs that. I had resolved that this was part of God's plan, and I wanted to be obedient to God no matter the cost. My spirit had said loudly: "Okay, God. Let's do this." I know it sounds like I was okay with losing Preston and that I didn't care if he lived or died, but that's the furthest thing from the truth. The fact is that I had finally come to the realization that, without God, we were both dead anyway. Maybe not in a physical sense, but that's all. Without Christ, we had begun to merely exist.

It was in those remaining moments on the long ride to the hospital when all the truths I had learned—all of God's promises, all of God's Word that I had been taught and that I had read about since becoming a Christian at age nine—began to repeat over and over in my head. What it all boiled down to, aside from what was happening in the moment, was that I needed God. I really had to rely on Him and trust Him, look for Him, listen for Him, seek Him, and praise Him as I'd never had to—and then stay in that mindset! Had there been desperate circumstances in my life before? Yes. Had I needed God before? Yes. Had I prayed to, listened to, followed, and praised Christ before? Yes. But this time it was different. I had never before experienced such an all-consuming, eerily sweet peace in the midst of life crumbling around me. I knew, even on the ride to the hospital, that my life was about to change completely. Without having a clue of the outcome, I knew that I, personally, would never be the same. I knew something was happening, and that I had to have my eyes, ears, and spirit wide open so that I wouldn't miss a minute of what God was going to do.

5

None of us had even remotely thought of the fact that we didn't know how to get to the hospital in Owensboro. It wasn't until we reached the city limits that one of us said we had no clue where we needed to be or how to get there. Talk about ironic. That statement described my life in general at that point.

Dad said he thought he knew the vicinity of the hospital, so he headed in that direction. As we were racing up and down side streets, looking for signs or indications of a hospital, I spotted a road construction worker. Now, let me make this clear. It was a Saturday morning on a back street, a side street, and there was one road worker standing on the sidewalk. No trucks, no other workers, no road work signs. Just one worker. I rolled down the window and, before we even reached this guy, I yelled, "Where is the hospital? How do I get to the hospital?" The gentleman quickly answered that we were very close and gave us directions for a couple of turns we needed to make.

We raced off before he was able to complete his last sentence.

Within seconds I could see the red "Emergency Room" sign and, before Dad could tell me any differently, I jumped out of the vehicle saying, "Park and bring the boys. I'm going in!" All I knew was that I could no longer wait to get through those automatic doors. I had to get to Preston.

As I entered, a kind gentleman with a friendly face met me at the door.

"Are you Mrs. Solise?"

"Yes. Yes, I am. I'm Karen."

The man introduced himself as someone who worked at the mines. Just as he finished, a doctor and a couple of nurses came rushing toward me. The doctor asked me the same thing: "Are you Karen?" After I answered him, the next few minutes began to kick into slow mode. It was as if I were in a bubble, watching movement around me. Words were all of a sudden a foreign language; the voices and movements around me became a rumble and a roar of background noise. I can still quote the doctor's first statement to me: "We have him stable, but as you can see by the team of people here and our rushing around, we just don't know if he will make it."

Honestly, I'm not sure whether the doctor said anything else to me. The next thing I remember is walking into the room where Preston was being treated. It was cold, bare, and lifeless. I'm not talking about the temperature or the décor. I'm talking about the feeling, the spirit, the presence; such a heaviness. Preston was lying flat on a table, strapped to the board the medical personnel had used to bring him in from the helicopter. He was wearing a neck brace and was covered with several wool hospital blankets to keep him warm. The only part of him that I could see was his face. His body was shaking uncontrollably. He would have small, consistent shivers and then intense, flailing, erratic movements, all the while murmuring and trying to open his eyes to see what was around him. I spoke to him as I approached his side and called his name. He recognized my voice and even tried to give me a small "hey." All the while, I remained constantly and indescribably calm.

Nurses began to share Preston's vital signs with me, along with what little information they had about the accident. I was in the room for only a few short minutes, until the doctor came in and told me they were going to take Preston so they could run more tests. The doctor assured me that he would keep me informed as quickly and routinely as he could. Before leaving the room, I leaned directly over Preston—like I was standing on my tippy toes to look down into a well (because of Preston's neck brace, I had to get high enough above the gurney to be in his line of vision)—and promised him I'd be waiting for him, and that I was going nowhere.

In no way was I prepared for what was to come next. Preston managed to gasp enough breath in his lungs to murmur to me for the first time since I'd gotten to him. And though it took a while to decode what he was saying, I finally deciphered it: "I prayed that I would die quickly."

I honestly hadn't thought that the room we were in could have gotten any colder, harder, heavier, staler, more sterile. But I was proven wrong instantly as Preston's murmur translated to words in my head. Yet we were about to receive a blessing—right at that very time, as the nurses wheeled Preston out of that cold, hard room and just as what Preston was saying was becoming clear to me. It was a blessing indeed, because the brutal truth of what had happened to Preston and what he had experienced flashed through my mind's eye as if I were watching a movie on a big screen with surround sound.

Preston had been folded in half (like a big taco, as he explains it—we compare everything to food) by the arms of the equipment, and he had thought his body was going to be cut in two. Those who were first on the scene told us later of how Preston's skin was wrinkled like a paper wad; they said over and over again that they couldn't describe how compact Preston was when they got to him. He was conscious throughout the entire ordeal, and he remembers, in detail, every motion, noise, and movement, every aspect of the accident. He was well aware of everything that was happening to him and around him, including his struggle to breathe and the intense pain that was consuming his body. Among many, many other injuries, his chest had been crushed, leaving him with little lung capacity. The pain radiating from his internal organs, collapsed lungs, and broken bones was nearly unbearable during the forty-minute ride out of the mines to the ground surface, as well as during the helicopter ride to the hospital.

If I had ever doubted that God controls all things—that He is present in every aspect of our lives and orchestrates events for His divine purpose—Christ removed that veil of deception piece by piece as this trial unfolded. One detail of this tragic event—one that may seem miniscule to some but is life-size in its significance—is the fact that one of the first people on the scene that morning in the mines was Preston's dear friend, Thad. He wasn't even supposed to be working that night, much less working directly with Preston during that particular shift. He was there only because he had been asked to cover for an absent worker. Thad had been mining with Preston throughout the course of their fourteen-year careers. He's a family friend—and he knows my parents.

When Thad got to Preston in the wee hours of the morning on April 10, 2004, only seconds after the accident, he immediately began to assess the situation, stabilize Preston, and make contact with those on the surface to arrange transportation out of the mines as quickly as possible. Thad held Preston's hand and prayed over him as they waited for help.

In the midst of managing the utter chaos, Thad could tell that Preston was trying to speak; that he was trying to communicate something. After listening intently as Preston made a few attempts, and as he himself kept trying to make sense of the sounds—"la, la, la"—Thad realized that Preston was trying to say "Larry."

My father's name.

Again, as God had orchestrated, Thad knew Preston so well that he knew my parents too. And that's why, and how, he was able to piece together that Preston wanted the mines staff to contact my dad, Larry, instead of calling me. Thad knew that Preston, not knowing if he would live to see the surface, wanted my dad to be the one to tell me about the circumstances and be with me and the boys. Selfless. Absolutely selfless.

It was in these moments—moments of uncertainty and chaos and pain—that God began to open my eyes, to open my heart, and teach me about Him. God's true character became so piercingly clear to me in those days, weeks, and months following the accident. I began to see, yet again in my life, God's endless mercy and grace and love. What was different this time? It was personal. I not only saw the acts of God, I saw the control of God. My teacher friends will understand when I say I experienced a deeper learning. I finally realized that God is not an unreachable God in Heaven, simply watching us. God is alive and well, reigning over all things, and He is actively involved in every intricate detail of our lives. Listen to this. Know this. Own this. God created the universe, and He controls it. Yet, He loves us enough to be attentive to every part of our lives. Christ is so madly, deeply in love with us that He wants only to share our lives with us; He wants to be included. God waits passively yet earnestly, desiring that we come to Him. Just as we know we are welcome in many situations but we prefer an invite just the same, God prefers an invite into our lives. I had set God on a shelf and had only dusted that shelf on occasion.

To say that this was the point in my life where I began to gain a better understanding of God would be an enormous understatement, and an injustice to the process of histolysis. Just as a caterpillar goes through the process of partial death, and some of its tissues are salvaged to form the new body, the me that had been created by the world was dying, and the me that Christ had created with intention was emerging. A relationship, one I had never previously experienced, was forming. A relationship that was more life-changing than the accident, the situation, or the circumstances.

Within a couple of hours of arriving at the red Emergency Room sign that day, I was able to take the boys to see their dad. After some testing, Preston had been placed back into the sterile, lifeless room where I had first seen him. I wanted our boys to see their dad for themselves. Since Preston's face was the only visible portion of his body and his pain level was being controlled by high levels of morphine, it seemed to be as opportune a time as any. I wanted Clay and Tanner to see that their dad was alive and to have the chance to talk with him. Even though I knew Preston would not be able to respond, and that he might not realize the boys were in the room, I felt it was important for them to have a few moments with him.

The responses from each of the boys were such a reflection of their respective personalities. Clay, who is more quiet and reserved, stood back at a distance. His discomfort was evident. He didn't want to get too close to his dad. His face portrayed his distress. Tanner, who is more open and direct, reacted in quite the opposite way. He sat on a stool as close as he could get to his dad's head on the gurney. He wanted to be as near to Preston as he could, and he wanted to see what was taking place. He didn't want to miss a thing as doctors and nurses popped in and out of the room continually to work with Preston.

Clay wanted to leave the room within seconds of entering. Tanner didn't want to leave his dad's side. But the pain on both of their faces revealed the same hurt and communicated the same message.

In the years since the accident, Clay and Tanner have both shared with us a few of their memories of it. Clay says he honestly didn't realize the severity of the situation until he got into the room with his dad. He says: "Of course, I almost passed out when I saw how hurt he was." I understand that sentiment completely; it was hard even for adults to see Preston, and none of us initially knew the severity of the accident. Clay also notes that, because he was only thirteen at the time, he had no idea how lucky he was to have his dad survive this type of accident and come back home eventually. "As I grew older," he says, "I was able to better understand the protecting and healing hand that was on him and our family. I have learned that to now be twenty-five, and to still have parents that are together and to have a family still together, makes me more rich than any monetary possession."

Tanner says that what stands out in his memory is how he felt when his dad couldn't play pitch and catch anymore. That was a big deal to him at ten years old. His dad had always done this with him, and it was hard to lose it. Tanner says that, at the time of the accident and in the months that followed, he was just plain angry. "Dad could always dunk and do cool stuff," he says. "Then, all of a sudden, he couldn't do anything. Not just sports, but anything. I was just starting to be at a point where I needed him to show me stuff, so I just had to figure things out on my own." Hearing Tanner say these things now hurts my core all over again.

The boys made many sacrifices after Preston's accident. One in particular was by Tanner. After being very sick and having yet another extended hospital stay, this time spending two weeks in the hospital in Denver, Tanner was finally beginning to experience what it was like to have his asthma under control. It was during that same time that Tan had expressed an interest in acting. Since Nashville was the closest place for Tanner to attain training and have opportunities for auditions, we made the commitment in 2002 to travel back and forth from our home in Kentucky to Nashville at least weekly.

After completing some training, Tanner ended up with three agents and began regularly going on auditions. He participated in events not only in the Nashville area but in other states as well. As 2004 began, Tanner was not only getting more auditions and parts, he had also been asked by one particular agent—in Hollywood—to submit several copies of recorded monologues. This same agent had even tossed out the idea of Tanner coming to Hollywood for pilot season. Things were moving quickly in that area of our lives, just like they were in every other area. Tanner was getting lots of attention and was becoming very busy with his schedule. As a matter of fact, our weekly one-hour-and-forty-five-minute (one way) trips to the other side of Nashville had become daily excursions. Yes, daily. And it went on for weeks.

Tanner had started doing print ads and commercials. Little did we know that all of the discussions and auditions would be halted abruptly through no fault of our own. It may have been yet another blessing in disguise. Tanner may not agree, but I can't help but believe it deep down—especially with the way it ended.

Tanner had been scheduled for an audition on the day of the accident. But in the chaos of the events, I completely forgot about it. I just wasn't able to focus on whether or not we were supposed to be anywhere that day. As soon as I'd arrived at the hospital, I'd gone into survival mode. I hadn't even brought my phone charger with me.

By the time Sunday evening rolled around and I began to think a bit more clearly, I realized what we had missed. So on Monday, after I'd asked someone to bring me my charger, I called the agent Tan would have been representing and told her about what had happened and why we had missed the audition.

It was not a pretty conversation.

The agent didn't care at all about our reason for missing the audition and was not happy with me in the least. Even though I described in detail what had happened and how severe the situation was—telling her I was in the hospital room with Preston at that very moment—she seemed to hear not a word I said. She was very clear on how she felt about us missing the audition, and she was adamant that she simply did not care what the reason was. She was furious. Even though we had two other agents and plenty of interest by both them and Tanner, we were never able to continue the acting pursuit.

The boys made many sacrifices; all of us did. And even though it's been years since we began our new normal, there are times when the impact is still so very fresh and the cut still so very deep.

—

After the boys had spent a few minutes with their dad, the doctor came in and told me that he had received the findings of the latest round of tests he had ordered. He asked that the boys return to the waiting room so that he could share the results with me. So the boys and my parents went off to wait again. As an adult, I have tried to regularly tell my parents how much I appreciate them, as they have been a constant in my life. But to this day, I'm not sure I've ever told them how much I appreciated them during this particular time—starting at 5:30 that Saturday morning.

After I heard about all the damage that had been done during the accident, nurses came to move Preston onto a hospital bed and into the Intensive Care Unit. As they prepared Preston for the move, I went to the waiting area, where numerous friends and family had gathered in support. It was then that I called my friend Libby—the one with whom I'd shared my gut feelings that something was about to unfold. I remember her exact words as they crawled from the other end of the line.

"Oh my, Karen. You said something was going to happen."

It was in that slow-motion, light bulb-burning, sun-rising, sky-opening moment when revelation came: The Holy Spirit had been speaking to me and had been preparing me for just a time as this. The Holy Spirit had interceded on my family's behalf. The God that I had put in a box on a shelf was revealing Himself, and I was FINALLY, TRULY, REALLY seeing Him. Christ was making Himself known to me in an intimate, personal way.

The first few days following the accident gave no indication as to how dramatically my perspective of religion would change. My reverence for Christ began to grow exponentially, while my mask of religion was diminishing in multiples. Lesson learned: The Holy Spirit is real.

Another truth I uncovered is that it's not religion with Christ that's important, but relationship with Christ. Merely adhering to a religion has no eternal significance. But a true, pure-hearted, personal relationship with Christ will reap the reward of eternal life. Hebrews tells us that we have a direct line to God and that the veil was lifted. In the weeks and months following the accident, Preston and I both watched and felt the sweet relief of our veils being lifted, personally and collectively. The removal of the veil of the world allowed our eyes and our hearts to see more clearly than we had in years. It was as if cataracts had been removed and our vision had been restored. And the amazing, wonderful, freeing truth is that Christ wants clear vision for everyone. No matter your circumstances, God wants to show you truth; real truth, eternal truth, His truth. Circumstances are simply that: things in our circumference, things around us. Our circumstances are NOT US. Your circumstances ARE NOT YOU. They are simply things around you.

One of the things I remember saying—several times—on the ride to the hospital was: "We have to find out who was operating the equipment. I have to find out. No one would do this intentionally. I have to let them know that this was just a terrible accident; no one is to blame. I cannot imagine how they are feeling. I want them to know that this was just an accident." I knew the other person had to be dealing with his own pain and devastation.

Because Preston was in Intensive Care for only one night and was then moved to a regular room, God gave me the opportunity to contact this person within the first couple of days following the accident. I am thankful to this day that I did not miss this chance and window of time. I wanted to close the door as quickly as I could slam it on Satan's chance to whisper lies to this gentleman. Even in the spiritual position I was in, God granted me the insight to know that Satan would take these events and twist and turn them into thoughts and emotions of hurt that could be buried for years, causing so much pain for everyone involved. If left alone and not dealt with immediately, the hurt, the pain, and the lies could have become yet another barrier in my relationship with Christ. God allowed me to state peace quickly, and I have since learned that doing so was as much for me as it was for the other person involved.

Now, Preston being in the ICU for only one night? That statement holds two miracles. One, having experienced what he had experienced, Preston should not have made it to the hospital alive in the first place. And two, his body should have been in such shock from his injuries that it needed more time and monitoring in Intensive Care. Remember: He had been pinned against a concrete-like wall of the mines, miles underground, by a two-ton piece of machinery.

As a matter of fact, the entire hospital stay was remarkably brief (six days) and fairly uneventful, all things considered. (I say FAIRLY uneventful because Preston's light above his bed did catch on fire one day.) As hospital stays go, this one was typical: continual vital checks, medicine dispensing, little to no sleep, and doctors visiting routinely. The only thing that seemed different: Each time the doctor came to see us, we learned of yet another injury, a newly discovered ailment or disability. Preston was so full of morphine (to manage the pain) that he simply couldn't gauge and/or express all the things that weren't right.

But there was something that had caught MY attention and had been lingering with me. Even while I was dealing with the initial shock of the accident on Saturday and was going through the motions to get settled in at the hospital for a bit, I had played it over and over in my head: how Preston's legs looked. They were lying in opposite directions; his feet and knees were pointing toward opposite sides of the room. Having no formal medical background, I'd spent the first several hours just trying to soak in what was happening. Even though I noticed Preston's legs even then, I think I was trying to convince myself that I was just overreacting and making something out of nothing. But on Sunday morning, as we awoke from one of our many dozing naps and prepared for the day, I was no longer capable of dismissing Preston's legs. They were limp, stationary, and immobile. The closer attention I paid to them, the more they looked as though they weren't even attached to his body.

I began making it a point to mention this to each nurse, doctor, therapist, and caregiver that came into Preston's hospital room, but the response I consistently received was: "We'll check on that." Well, finally, on Monday, when physical therapy staffers came to Preston's room to get him up and out of bed for the first time, we all realized that the doctors had no choice but to do further checking on Preston's legs. Once the two therapists had placed a harness around Preston's waist and were in the midst of working collectively to help him stand, they saw that his legs were unstable and therefore incapable of holding his body. At that very same time, we all heard an enormous popping noise. The therapists immediately started saying: "Sit him down. Sit him down now!"

The therapist who had been holding the back of the harness had also placed his hand on Preston's lower back. He said that, just as he'd begun to try and lift Preston, he'd felt a bone protrude from Preston's lower back. Finally—someone else had a suspicion that Preston's legs, hips, or pelvis (or all three) had injuries that had not yet been identified. The therapists asked Preston to remain in his bed and not try to stand again until further notice. They then went directly to the doctor in charge and requested that more X-rays be completed. Within a few hours, Preston was once again taken to the radiology department in hopes that his body's swelling had declined and that new X-rays would offer clearer pictures of what was going on. And it was with this round of scans that we discovered that all of the muscles, tendons, and ligaments had been torn from Preston's pelvis—which confirmed that it hadn't been an illusion I'd been seeing. Preston's legs weren't fully attached as normal.

———

We didn't learn about all of Preston's injuries at once. More injuries became evident as Preston's pain grew more intense. From the beginning, we had known of the damaged left arm, the broken clavicle, the broken sternum, and the collapsed lungs. But we would slowly learn of more injuries and have more cause for alarm. The progression of time would also reveal the unbearable pain these injuries brought with them.

Preston's left arm had nerve damage; it was limp and hung at his side due to the crushing of his shoulder. All of its muscles, tendons, and nerves had been flattened beyond repair by regeneration. Along with the broken clavicle, broken sternum, and collapsed lungs, Preston had all of the ligaments torn from his pelvis, broken ribs, and numerous deep bruises. When he was released from the hospital, he was unable to walk—and he hadn't been weaned from the high amounts of morphine he'd been on since entering the ER on Saturday. He was also learning of even more injuries daily.

And that's where the nightmare truly began.

Shortly after we got back home, Preston's morphine began to wear off. So I gave him the pain medicine that had been prescribed to us for use at home.

Little did we know that Preston's body would not accept these meds.

He began vomiting, and the medicine didn't ease his pain in the least. As his pain intensified, so did his screams. His body completely rejected this very high-level, typically potent medication; it did nothing but make him throw up and writhe in pain. Imagine vomiting while your whole body is dealing with numerous injuries and intense pain. Seeing Preston like this was horrific. I had never experienced anything like it; I had never seen anyone in such agony. He was screaming, begging me to call the pharmacist, thinking he'd been given a placebo. I called every pharmacist I knew. They each assured me that the medication prescribed was the strongest possible and that it couldn't be changed without a doctor's order.

This horror went on for several days, until the doctor was able to be contacted. He acknowledged that Preston's body was rejecting the medication and ordered a different pain medication.

Seeing Preston go through that torment and torture is something I will never forget. His nightmares were about the accident; mine were about watching him suffer. Over the course of one short week, I had seen the person I had given my heart to go from being a vibrant, athletic, strong, active man to someone whose body I was bathing, whose teeth I was brushing, whose hair I was shampooing. I was clothing him and feeding him too, all while listening to him wail in pain. I cannot discount the boldness, determination, strength, and peace that God encased over me at that time. With the help of God, I took control and did what needed to be done and kept peace and positivity all the while.

Unfortunately, though, managing Preston's pain took more than a simple switching of medicines. Getting it under control required trying several medication combinations over the course of several days of unprecedented, uninhibited cries for mercy. Again, this is where our journey truly began. It was in our daily living AFTER the accident when we encountered the biggest struggles.

Going home from the hospital began months and months of intense rehabilitation. I watched as Preston fought from my having to feed him to, months later, being able to fix his own plate of food, carry it with one arm to his place at the family table, and feed himself. He approached the entire rehabilitation journey with this same methodical, determined mentality. He would pick one thing that he wanted to be able to do again, one obstacle, and go full force until he had overcome. Months after the accident, he had finally conquered the laundry! He had to carry one piece of clothing at a time from the hamper to the washer, then one piece from the washer to the dryer, and then one piece from the dryer to the sofa for folding, but he did it! It took all day for him to finish one load, but he did it!

It's interesting to me that this is one of the victories I remember so distinctly, but it was nearly a year after the accident before

Preston could actually sit in a chair. He kept trying, kept inching, kept fighting, and eventually he did it. He went to rehab three times each week and did all the home exercises the therapists recommended. God sustained us—minute by minute, day by day.

After MONTHS of rehab, God revealed to us the answer to the burning question that had been on my mind since the morning of the accident: Why, when Preston had been asked where he wanted to be taken as he was being carried out from underground, had he mustered up the mentality and lung capacity to say, "Owensboro"? After the months had passed and Preston's left arm was still simply hanging and unable to be used, the doctors came to accept the fact that the nerves were not going to regenerate themselves; Preston would need reconstructive surgery if he was ever to use his arm again. There were no guarantees, but the only thing left to try was the surgery. Little did we know that the orthopedic doctor to whom we had been referred there in Owensboro (by the doctor initially on the case from the time Preston was unloaded from the life flight) had worked with an internationally known surgeon who specializes in nerve transfer and reconstruction. What are the chances that a doctor in Owensboro, Kentucky, under whose care we were randomly placed by the initial doctor, would know a surgeon with this exact expertise? Dr. Susan MacKinnon CREATED the surgery she performed on Preston's arm and hand. She CREATED it! THAT IS GOD! Dr. MacKinnon was literally a godsend; she was the hands of God for Preston. We knew it the minute we met with her for consultation. With all the knowledge and accolades she had accumulated, she was so in tune to

Preston—his pain and his hurt, which were two very different things. Though the physical pain was relentless and excruciating, the mental hurt was just as difficult to endure at times.

In the months following the accident, we had all begun to face the new normal for us as a family. But Preston seemed to be the one trapped inside the pain and hurt. One of the most difficult changes for me to accept as things unfolded was the fact that Preston would no longer be able to offer hugs with two arms. My boys would never feel the complete embrace of their dad having both arms wrapped tightly around them. I cried endlessly in the shower just trying to deal with the injustice that Preston would never hug me as he once had. There would be no more playing ball with Dad, no more wrestling on the living room floor, no more walks around our little town. There would be many things the boys and I would have to do for ourselves now that were once simple acts of love and caretaking. Our boys had to immediately become the men of the house at the ages of thirteen and ten, and they seemed to welcome their new responsibilities. From the time Preston had been moved to his regular room at the hospital, both Clay and Tanner had been very tuned in to his needs, his limitations, and his pain. As young as they were, they were both so very willing to help me or their dad in any way they could. They realized that Preston simply could not do anything physical. For months, it was a task for him to simply get himself to and from the restroom. So one day our boys were carefree—playing video games, participating in sports, hanging out with friends who would come and go in our home; the next day the boys were having to help with landscaping, lawn mowing, and all household chores that required any lifting and/or fixing. Before the accident, the boys constantly had friends over; kids were running in and out of the house and spending the night. After the accident, we had to try to keep our home calm and quiet. Noise and lots of activity made it harder for Preston to rest and focus on healing, especially when he was in so much pain. The sudden change in the culture of our home—the immediate halt in activity—was the most difficult adjustment for our sons to face. But both Clay and Tanner stepped up and became little caretakers. As a matter of fact, when Preston did begin to try and move about the house without his wheelchair, even to get a drink or go to the restroom, the boys were so protective of him. They kept their eyes on him like hawks. To this day, as I think of how they stepped up, it makes me so very proud of them all over again.

We went from being very active and on the go to a complete halt. We were confined to our home, and the atmosphere inside became stale and heavy. Preston was accustomed to playing sports with the boys. Whether he's been out in our driveway shooting hoops with them or in the yard taking batting practice with them, Preston has always been very active and hands on in our boys' lives. There were many things my perceptions could skew when it came to Preston's role as a husband, but his role as a father has never been questionable. He is a remarkable daddy. Heck, this is a guy who coached football for boys in the first and second grades before we ever had children of our own.

So the boys and I learned to take on new roles and challenges. All the while, Preston was battling back as hard as he could. But his arm and hand just wouldn't make any progress without surgical intervention.

So in August 2004, Preston had surgery in St. Louis to reconfigure the nerves in his left arm and hand. His doctor rerouted the nerves so that the one nerve that did function in Preston's arm could have the chance to operate his entire arm and hand, as if the three nerves that should exist were really functioning normally. Again, this surgeon was the hands of God; this was nothing less than a miracle. As Dr. MacKinnon visited us in the pre-op waiting area, our pastor at the time (who was also a dear friend) was with us. Dr. MacKinnon asked if the gentleman was our pastor—and whether she could join us if we were going to have prayer. The uncertainty of the long, tedious surgery was calmed by that request. Preston and I both knew that God had work to do on him through this surgeon; and that He did.

After a painful recovery, many trips back and forth to St. Louis, and yet more therapy, Dr. MacKinnon's projection of progress was spot on. She had told Preston before the surgery that IF it was successful, it would be nine months before we would know whether the nerves would operate his *hand*. In other words: Even though, within two to three months, we would see a change in Preston's *arm* in that he would be able to lift it to an extent, it would be nine full months before we'd know whether the surgery would enable his *hand* to open.

Preston's hand had remained in a closed, drawn position since the accident. In April 2005, eight months after the surgery, we shared with our Sunday School class our prayer that Preston's hand would open and that he would regain some strength and use in his arm and hand. The surgery was showing no signs of success where his hand was concerned, and we were getting more and more anxious as the nine-month mark approached. Little did we know that this would be just another way that God would show Himself worthy of praise: all-knowing, in control, holy. Our Sunday School teacher, David Jones—who had called Preston nearly daily since the accident and had been the one to get him through many trying days—later shared with us that it was at this time, in late April and early May, when he began to doubt the success of the surgery. He told us he had prayed for Preston one night as he had done many times before—except that this time, he'd prayed God would give us the strength to accept things as they were, because he was coming to the belief that there would be no change in Preston's hand. He, as we had at times, had felt that there should have been some sign of improvement to this point, and that there had been none. The outlook was grim.

But God.

By the middle of May, one year and one month after the accident, Preston had begun to drive a little more often, and he would simply place his left arm on the steering wheel. One day, he went to pick up the boys from school. He was driving down the road, not focusing on his hand, when he noticed something: As it lay on top of the steering wheel, it began to open involuntarily. He told me he had been so shocked by what was going on that he'd kept watching to be sure he was really seeing his hand open. He couldn't believe it! In picking up the boys and coming back home, Preston had uncovered our entertainment for the night: We watched over and over again as his hand would open involuntarily—and then as he would concentrate so intently to get his hand to operate *on command*. God was performing a miracle right in our living room.

Initially, Preston and I sat with all of this for hours, not saying a word, in shock about the presence and power of Christ. But when we started praising, WE PRAISED! Preston showed off everywhere we went, to anyone who would watch. We began by showing what was going on to our Sunday School Class, then the church body, then anyone and everyone wherever we went: grocery store, school, errands, whatever. We wanted to be sure to share our miracle with everyone. We didn't want to pass someone who might have been waiting for their miracle, just as we had waited. Know this: There are things God is doing in your life that need to be shared. You have a story.

When we went to our scheduled follow-up appointment in early June, Dr. MacKinnon was thrilled to see that Preston's nerves were working as they should and that the surgery was a success. At this point, we were elated to simply have the hand operating. But that evolved into a next step: Pray for strength within Preston's hand. And so we began.

Please notice that I continually use the pronoun "we." That's how it was. Preston did not go through this experience alone. He wasn't the only one affected, nor did the journey require only his energy. We were in it together: every aspect, every challenge, every victory. Preston began working, pushing, fighting, and I began praying and supporting alongside. We were specific in our prayers and intentional in our commitment to prayer. We needed God to continue working in our lives, which meant we had to continue seeking Him and follow. And just as always, God, in His faithfulness, moved on our behalf.

We returned for the next check-up later in June, and Dr. MacKinnon was so very pleased with the progress Preston had made in only a few weeks. During this visit we were once again able to proclaim what had transpired as work from the hand of God. We shared with our doctor and all of her staff, every opportunity we got, that it was God who had brought us to her, God who had worked through her hands during the surgery, God who had blessed us with the healing that had come. We did not want to take for granted that any of the people we were in contact with knew God or His power. We did not want God's work to go unnoticed or unknown.

———

Given the hours, days, weeks, and months of struggle physically and mentally, not to mention the financial burdens that had come to us and the overwhelming mounds of continuous paperwork, it seemed we faced new obstacles every day. Not only were we dealing with issues minute by minute, we also had to continually prove our physical and financial status with documentation. Plus, each time we would progress with rehabilitation, there would be some new injury discovered, some new ailment, some necessary medicine change. Workers' Compensation would decide not to cover a medication any longer; Preston's body would become immune to a medicine; a medicine would bring more harmful side effects than benefits: There were constant changes. There were so many factors at work that I cannot even begin to name them all.

I remember the anguish of watching Preston suffer, the heartache of seeing him struggle with tasks we take for granted—simple things like washing his hair (it was tough for him to hold the shampoo bottle with his one working hand, put shampoo in that same hand, and then lather), drying off with a towel after a shower, pouring a drink while holding the glass, fixing himself a plate while holding the plate, taking medicine on his own (including being able to open the medicine bottle or box). These were but a few of the activities that became monumental challenges for Preston.

I remember watching him learn to dress himself with one arm and one hand. I remember having to put his socks on him and tie his shoes for him. We eventually bought shoes that didn't require tying so that he could dress himself completely during his rehabilitation period. I remember watching him chase food on his plate because of his limitation to one arm and hand. I remember how it hurt him to hear others talking about their work, no matter what industry they were in, because all he wanted was to go back to work himself.

The financial impact of Preston's accident was also tremendous. Our income had been cut by one-third. We could no longer contribute to our retirement, nor was Preston's employer contributing to it as before. But we never missed a bill or a meal. We did not direct our energy toward money. We completely let God handle our finances, and He provided at every turn. One particular instance stands out to me. We were low on funds, and we had just received our vehicle insurance bill. We needed some groceries as well. For the first time, we were going to have to make a seemingly impossible decision: We could either not get the groceries and pay the vehicle insurance in full, or we could pay only a portion of the insurance bill so that we'd still be able to get the groceries. As I said, Preston and I had concluded that we would completely let God take care of our finances. He had gotten us this far, and we knew He wouldn't let go of us now. Preston and I discussed the situation very briefly and simply prayed together that God would direct us as to what to do. The next day—the very next day—we received a refund check from our local medical center in an amount almost identical to the amount we needed for the insurance bill. OH, YES WE DID! Or better yet: OH, YES *HE* DID! And that's all I'll say about that. The uphill climb became laden with loads of weights to carry and factors pushing against us. But God. God continually revealed His power and presence in our lives. Every time things began to push against us, God proved to be bigger.

Here's another example of when God blew our minds with His provision, as well as His grace in working within us. One day in March 2005, the sun was shining and I was headed outside to do some spring chores: exterior painting around the house, cleaning the landscape, yard work, etc. As I walked through our back door to go through our garage on my way outside, I had a very real, very clear experience when God spoke to me and the Holy Spirit moved over me. Yes, I was walking through my garage. And yes, it may seem like the most unlikely place for Christ to speak to me. But yes, it happened.

As my feet stepped off the concrete steps leading into our back door and onto the concrete floor of our vehicle storage space, God made me very aware that we would be getting a new vehicle. WHAT? Preston is injured, still recovering from reconstructive surgery on the nerves in his arm and hand, and our only income is my teaching salary plus one-third of Preston's base salary. Did I hear correctly?

At first I was surprised. Well, let's be real: I was SHOCKED. But when this thought came over my spirit, I immediately sat and soaked in the presence of God. I wanted to see if there was more to come, if God was going to say more, and I sensed it was a time to simply be quiet and let God's vision come into focus. So as I sat in silence on the concrete of my driveway, peace came over me while God helped me process and accept that He was going to bless us again. Now, get this: God was not blessing us so that we would just accept His blessings and hold onto them. Nor was He blessing us so that we could be seen, or so that we could show what we had gotten. God was blessing us so that *He* could be seen, and so that we could give Him the glory.

Clay was a freshman in high school and Tanner was in middle school at this point. Through our continuing efforts to keep things as normal as possible, the boys were both active in sports, and we were transporting them and their friends all over our county and the surrounding counties for various athletic events. Remember: Preston and I had decided to share our story with everyone who would listen. We wanted people to know that God had spared Preston's life, and that He was restoring Preston's body through rehabilitation, medicine, and the direction of great doctors and caregivers. But we wanted people to realize as well that things still weren't perfect—nowhere near—nor were they improving quickly. We wanted others to see how God was blessing us to accept, act on, and react to all the events in our lives. Our biggest stand was that God was, is, and always will be faithful.

How does all of this connect to God providing us with a new vehicle? Well, we didn't want to witness only to adults. We wanted to be a witness to our kids, to their friends, and to their families, too. We wanted to spend time with our boys' friends and speak into their lives. Preston and I both had vehicles that seated only five, and with our growing boys and their friends, the five had become four if we wanted to fit comfortably.

So God gave us an SUV that seated eight.

We both, to this very day, stand by the perspective that God provided this vehicle. The entire situation was so laid out by God that we couldn't have ignored the path even if we'd tried. When God spoke to me in our garage that day and I sat listening, the details of what we were to do were given specifically, including the dealership we were to go to and the salesperson we were to speak to. Beyond that, I didn't know what God had planned for us. But I knew we were to go to that specific salesperson and that we would learn.

And so we did. We went to the dealership and met with the gentleman God had revealed to me. We shared our situation, telling him that Preston wasn't working and that we wanted to be able to tote lots of stinky ball players. The salesman's response was amazing: The dealership had on hand an SUV that had just been traded in—one priced so low that he himself could not believe it. He said it would be perfect for us. And so it was. As we walked out to the car lot and approached the vehicle, Preston and I simply looked at one another and literally laughed. The peace was evident, and we knew without looking any further that this was what God had led us to. We asked the salesperson to excuse us, opened the door of the vehicle, and prayed together, asking God to guide our steps in the matter and thanking Him for His presence in our lives. We thanked God that He would choose to speak to us and communicate with us. We then walked into the dealership with the salesperson and had the smoothest transaction we have, to this day, ever experienced in buying a vehicle. No offense to anyone, but we all know that it typically takes lots of time to make this type of purchase. But on this particular occasion, we concluded the entire transaction and left the dealership within an hour. God did that. From beginning to end, God did that. And we kept that vehicle through both of our boys' high school careers.

There's more. God used this same vehicle again two years ago to bless us in yet another way: We were able to sell it to finance our oldest son's opportunity to fulfill a lifelong dream. During his senior year of college, we were able to help Clay move to Boston and work on the production team for the Boston Red Sox. Clay has been a fan of the Red Sox since he could walk, and he had always wanted to go to Fenway Park. God gave him the blessing of not only going to Fenway, but being able to step onto the field there. God's love, grace, mercy, and abundance have no end.

PLEASE do not get caught up on the vehicle itself; this wasn't about the vehicle, not in any way. It was all about God. It is all about God, His power, and His goodness. It's about how God wants to work in our lives, IF only we let Him. This was one of the times we learned that when you think there is no way, God will make a way. Christ wanted others to see that He was not merely providing for us, but blessing us beyond our needs. He was providing above and beyond. It's all for His glory, after all. It's not about Christ giving us things we want or making things easier for us. It's about us following His lead and being obedient to His purpose, His voice, His will. I missed that message for so, so long. My heart yearns for you to hear the real story behind these events. It's all about God and our heart's relationship with Him—nothing else.

While he'd been in the hospital following the accident, Preston had been told he would never be able to work again, and that he might not be able to walk again either. So even though he was now indeed walking and had regained some use of his arm and hand, there were times I tried to prepare him for the idea that he would never return to work. But he would have nothing to do with entertaining these thoughts. He stuck to his perspective that God was going to send him not only back to work, but back to work in the same coal mines where the accident had happened. He stood his ground that God WOULD use his experience as a testimony (and so it continues to be).

Are you ready for this? Are you sitting down? After seventeen months of grueling recovery and rehabilitation, Preston returned to work in the same mines where the accident had occurred. If he'd needed more than eighteen months to recover, he would have lost his job. But God. God saw fit to bring Preston to a point where he could work. At the seventeen-month mark, Preston had regained as much use of and strength in his arm and hand as he was going to get back. And even though he was not, nor would he ever be, one hundred percent as he was prior to the accident, two years after he was crushed his determination and God's grace allowed him to return to coal mining and work for almost ten years after that life-changing accident.

Just as I had always seen my classroom as my mission field, Preston had always seen the underground mines as his. He took full advantage of his return and witnessed to anyone and everyone around. The majority of the time he did so without saying a word. Everyone knew his story, and for the new ones who didn't, he was always willing to share what God had brought him through. More so than that, Preston's work ethic spoke volumes. There were numerous times when his co-workers told me he worked harder than men with two arms—men who hadn't been crushed. Preston took pride in working hard in order to show Christ to others. Just as Colossians 3:23 states: "Whatever you do, work at it with all your heart, as working for the Lord, not for human masters." Though tired, he remained a witness at his workplace and talked with co-workers about Jesus at every opportunity.

Remember when I said that things were fairly uneventful immediately following Preston's hospital stay? Well, I want to elaborate on that. Yes, Preston had just survived being crushed in a mining accident. Yes, he'd had a short stay in the Intensive

Care Unit. And yes, his room light had caught on fire before he had been moved away without harm.

There's more.

God was not going to stop working in our lives, but Satan was not going to stop trying to intervene either. On the day Preston was released from the hospital, he couldn't walk, and he was in a brace due to his cracked collarbone and numerous other broken bones. He had plenty to deal with as it was. When we had gotten about twenty minutes away from the hospital, a large rock truck came toward us from the opposite direction. As the truck passed us, a HUGE rock either fell from the truck or was thrown up from under its wheel. It came directly at Preston's side of the windshield. The rock hit the windshield with a tremendously loud impact and busted the glass directly in front of, and at the exact level of, Preston's face. It happened so quickly and with such a bang that we were both startled and shaken. As our reflexes kicked in, we both tensed up with the impact, which only added to Preston's pain level. I remember him simply whispering: "Please just get me home."

There's more.

After Preston had been vomiting and battling his excruciating pain for a while since coming home, it was time for him to return to his doctor for a follow-up appointment. At that point, we were still trying to find a mixture of medications that would offer any element of relief, and we hadn't yet succeeded. Since he was in such pain, it took time for us to get him settled into the car and into a position he found manageable. To make matters worse, we had to go back to Owensboro, a little over an hour from our home. Let's just say that car rides were extremely difficult for Preston.

We had just left home on this particular trip and were going around the lake in front of our house. As we approached a small hill, a truck going well over the speed limit came over the hill on our side of the road, nearly hitting us head on. I immediately slammed on the brakes and steered the car off the side of the road. Preston and I were both in complete disbelief. If we had been any closer to that hill, we would have been in a head-on collision. We sat there stunned for a few minutes, briefly entertaining the idea of simply turning around and going back home. I think it was apparent to us that the devil was not going to give in easily—and that, whether we wanted it or not, we were in the ring with him again for our next round.

I could write endlessly about the injuries, the obstacles, the hardships, the pain, the injustice, the barriers; the months, weeks, days, hours of rehab; the changes that resulted from this accident. But that is not my purpose in writing; these aren't the things I want to focus on or portray. What I do want to communicate clearly is that I had made my choices, and my choices had made me.

Long before the accident, I should have examined myself, my attitude, my heart. I was so engrossed in my "doing" that I forgot about my "being." What I see now is that I should have taken the time to be still, to reflect—to take a clear, honest, real look at myself. Instead, I gave power to those thoughts, those whispers, and those lies from Satan. Yes, I gave them power. You see, among the many things I have learned is that I have to be very vigilant about and mindful of what I give with respect to my time, my attention, my thoughts, and my energy—because with all of these things I give control and power; I give myself. Before Preston's accident, I had completely given the world around me the power to control me. The result? A mere existence of robotic motion. I had bought into the lie that life was just going to be that way, but that is the furthest thing from God's truth!

Had I been real with myself, and had I been brutally honest about my relationship with Christ, I would have come to the realization that I had allowed my relationship with God to go only so far—to an extent that was fairly superficial. Had I done a heart check, I would have embraced and cherished many more beautiful moments and experienced so much more joy and fulfillment in my early adult life. My life could have had such a different impact during those wandering years if only I hadn't seen God as a faraway entity that existed only to bring salvation and serve as a Savior. Praise God I now know the TRUTH! My God is a God of abundance, and peace, and grace, and mercy. My God is my Savior, Redeemer, Friend, Abba, Father, Healer, Prince of Peace, Advocate—my guide, my Lord. I no longer see Christ as my banker, to whom I go to make deposits and withdrawals on an as-needed basis. Christ is my continual companion, the longing of love and desire of good within me. I urge you to take a true, real, deep, honest look at your heart, your attitude, and your choices. Are you missing true fulfillment? Does peace escape you? How is your personal relationship with God?

I was about to throw away my world because of my feelings, my emotions. Know this: Emotions are fleeting. I was deceived by my own selfish emotions. I was doing so much for others (our youngest son had been sick for five-plus years at that point, I was teaching, coaching, taking college classes) and giving so much of myself that I had, as Lysa TerKeurst refers to it, no white space. I had nothing left in me. Every inch of my being, my existence, was drained. I had allowed myself to go beyond bankrupt physically, spiritually, and emotionally; my account was overdrawn. This left me with only the feelings and the emotions—deep, desperate emotions that directed me to see fantasy. Because I lacked true connections with anyone, and because I had filled my real world with schedules and to-do lists and demands, my mind led me to a fantasy world. My mind devised what I thought SHOULD be going on in my life. This plan created expectations that only I knew, and that was one root of the problem.

Preston and I had never talked about our expectations, our needs as a couple, our needs as individuals, or areas where we needed extra help. (YES, we ALL need extra help from time to time—that's reality!) Our lives were crammed with commitments to things outside our family and home that had impacted, strained, and overshadowed our commitments to one another and the children, the home, and the blessed life God had given us. We had given God no choice but to get our attention. I never cease to praise God because he chose to act in love—to get our attention and redirect us. Yes, I said that. I thank God continually that he got our attention. Am I saying that God caused

Preston's accident? No. Am I saying that I'm thankful Preston was injured? No. HECK NO. But am I saying that, through this accident, God saved our living? YES. ABSOLUTELY!

Preston being crushed in a dark place under the earth and being brought to the surface, only to shock doctors, healthcare providers, friends, family, and us—the whole experience is in such alignment with, and it is such a metaphor for, where we were spiritually at the time. Through this trial, God crumbled us of ourselves, raised us to His light, nurtured us to a true relationship with Him, changed us and made us new, individually and as a couple. God does NOT want us to have a superficial relationship with Him. Preston and I were Christians, believers, saved souls, before April 10, 2004. We had both accepted Christ as our Savior and had accepted salvation, so God had saved our souls, our lives, already. But through Preston's accident and its aftermath, God saved our living. He brought us back to life and stopped our mere existence. He made us alive to where we could see His presence, see His hands at work, see His control and protection and blessings, even in hardships. Christ opened our eyes to the meaning of living in His abundant, power-filled grace and mercy-filled fullness of life. God allowed us to see that our circumstances do not define us and that the weight of this world is not ours to carry. We are only to give our burdens to God and find rest in Him. We just didn't get it before. We saw the here and now. We were oblivious to the eternal significance of daily encounters here on Earth. Yes, every day offers encounters with Christ. He is constantly at work. We can choose to ignore this fact and live beneath our means, or we can choose to join Him and be an instrument for His work. I step out in boldness to say that too many of us, even Christians, are living beneath what God wants for our lives. God wants to bless us with abundant peace, joy, love, grace, and mercy; it is our choice to accept.

One of my favorite quotes comes from an evangelist named Ken Freeman: "We are all just one choice away from a different life." I shudder to think of my life had God not intervened. My emotional choices would have destroyed me, and I would have had only myself to blame. I would have allowed a single season of life to direct my entire harvest.

You might think that it's easy for me to say these things, since I wasn't the one injured, forever scarred—the one whose life was altered until death. But Preston will tell you the same thing. He has said from the beginning that he would not change or take back the accident. "It has made me a better person," he stresses—even though he still deals with the physical pain and limitations to this very day.

*L*ooking back, I know God wasn't surprised by what was happening in our lives or by what choices we were making. But I can see clearly, now, the opportunities He had given us to change our direction before Preston's accident. Even though we didn't find our own way out, and Christ had to guide us a bit, He has still allowed messages and testimonies to come from such a mess and a test. I believe, with all of my being, in the scripture of John 16:33 that states: "I have told you these things, so that in me you may have peace. In this world you will have trouble. But take heart! I have overcome the world." I also love the forty-third book of Isaiah. My favorite scripture from that book is Isaiah 43:2: "When you pass through the waters, I will be with you; and when you pass through the rivers, they will not sweep over you. When you walk through the fire, you will not be burned; the flames will not set you ablaze."

God can and will use our junk, our hardships, our trials to create opportunities for greatness to further His Kingdom—if we choose to perceive things that way and allow God to work. If we allow ourselves to accept the bravery, the boldness, and the faith God has planted within us when we accept Him as our Savior, He begins to live within us.

We each have access to bravery, boldness, faith, and power that can change not only our own lives, but others' lives as well—the world around us. But Christ, being the gentleman He is, doesn't force Himself upon us. We must actively and purposefully choose to access the power of Christ within us. I missed this mark for so long. Trust me: I am nowhere near where I need to be in my walk. I miss chances to share Christ, I allow fear to hush the spirit stirring within me, and, too many times, I go through my day beneath the threshold of joy and abundance given to me. But I am better than I was, and each day I'm making conscious efforts to walk closer with Christ, become more Christ-like, seek God in every aspect of my day, and share the blessings God has given me. I seek to be real, honest, transparent, and deeply in love with God and my life. God doesn't expect perfection. He simply wants us to give our best—just as we as parents do not expect perfection from our children but want their best efforts. Just as we as parents want only good for our children, God wants so much more for us. Just as we as parents want to be a part of our children's lives no matter their age, God wants to be included in our lives. We have made things much more complicated than God ever intended. Many of the ideas, traditions, and thought processes we tend to follow today are manmade rules and expectations; they're not based on scripture. That's why it's so important for us to take time to read God's word, talk with Him, listen as He speaks to us, and seek Him in every aspect of our lives. We must follow what Christ says, not what we as men have created: rules, boundaries, expectations, and guidelines that suit us. God appreciates simple; it's all about our hearts.

So for Preston and me, the pinning of mining equipment, the journey through rehabilitation, the disabilities and the scars that remain from April 10, 2004—they're all blessings.

—

Are you like I was, blinded by the things of this world? The truth is that we can strive, reach, grab, fight, push, or pull; have money, homes, toys, things, property, job titles, fame, recognition, even world-renowned accomplishments. But none of it will fulfill that one yearning deep within you, the one you maybe can't explain. You can travel or stay at home; you can work for a Fortune 500 company or from your kitchen table; you can save every dime you earn or give lavishly to those in need; you can choose to serve others or work to be the best person you can possibly become. NONE of these things will fill the hole or void that, no matter what you do, still exists. You can be in the best season of your life or in the depths of a pit you helped create. You may be wealthy or flat broke. You may be in a content position or you may be in the depths of despair you can't seem to escape. You may be suffering from pain your heart can no longer manage. You may feel you're in a situation that no one understands or cares about.

Are you weary and worn? Do you feel like you don't have the energy to expend any more effort on anything? Well, here are some solid truths you need to hear no matter where you are, no matter what you've done, no matter what you're suffering from, no matter how things look at this moment:

God knows.

God cares.

God is there with you.

Call upon God and you WILL see change. Do not give lip service to this one. Do not call on Jesus half-heartedly. Do not voice his name without belief. I'm talking about down in the very depths of who you are, with every fiber of your being: Call on the name of the Lord. Let Him know you need Him. Express your heart of belief to Him—that you believe in Him, and that you believe He can reach you, rescue you, sustain you, deliver you, rejuvenate you, redeem you, and recover you. HE WILL COME TO YOU! HE WILL SET YOU FREE!

One of the many things I've learned on my journey over the last eleven years is that when we seek God, we find God. There is nowhere you or I can hide from Christ, nowhere you or I can run from His love. God is wherever you are, including the pit you've jumped or fallen into. Call to Him. He will lift you out and plant you on firm ground. God is our only hope.

This may be your response: "Oh, Karen, you don't know what I'm dealing with." You're right; I don't. But God does. Or "you don't know what I've done." Again, you're right; I don't. But God does. Or "you can say these things because you haven't suffered what I have suffered." That is correct. But God knows it all, He sees it all, AND He wants to bear it all just FOR YOU. Whatever your situation, circumstances, or choices, let me be crystal clear: What I think, how much I know, my view, my opinion—none of it matters. My sin is no different from your sin, period. The Bible, God's word, is very clear on this. A sin is not measured by impact; that perception is manmade. God is the one to judge. And because God knew we were going to sin, He was born unto Mary so that He could die and bear all of our sins on the cross of Calvary. The perceptions others have of us, the hurt we experience (whether it is self-inflicted or brought on by circumstance or someone else), the extent or depth of our flaws—none of it matters to Christ. He wants to release us of all those things and give us freedom and new life through Him.

Another truth: Though we all need Christ and need to be saved, Christ would have died for you even if you'd been the only one who needed Him. I encourage you, I urge you: Just whisper the name of Jesus and begin anew. God can and will do for you what He did for Preston and me early that April morning, and what He continues to do for us as a couple. If you are willing to let Him, HE WILL CARRY YOU OUT OF THE DARKNESS.

⟶

In discussing what we each learned from going through the trials of Preston's accident, to say nothing of what we've learned since, Preston and I decided to make a list of the top things we know to be true from our experience. Once we began to read our respective responses to one another, we found that our lists were nearly identical. It sounds like a cliché, but words simply cannot do justice to what we have learned and the value of these lessons. The quality of our lives, though diminished so greatly in some respects, has increased tenfold in others. Here are just a few of the things Preston and I wrote down as to what this adversity has taught us—and is still teaching us:

God is always in control.

When you think there is no way, God makes a way.

Trust.

Faith.

Patience.

Take it all in.

Time is precious.

Relax and enjoy.

All of the Bible is TRUTH.

Respect—God, myself, each other, others.

Empathy, sympathy.

Be real—be me.

Walk in God's plan—let go of control.

Be the church.

Praise and truly worship.

Perspective.

Count it all a joy.

Armor up.

Psalm 28:7: "The Lord is my strength and my shield. I trust Him with all my heart. He helps me, and my heart is filled with joy. I burst in songs of thanksgiving."

The Holy Spirit is REAL.

There is power in me.

Pray AND listen.

God is always in control. There have been numerous times in my life, thinking back to a young age, when I thought God wasn't listening to me, that He didn't hear me, that He wasn't there, that He was ignoring me, that maybe He just didn't even care about me at all because I couldn't see Him answering my prayers when I wanted Him to and/or the way I wanted Him to. My view was simple: I didn't know God intimately and therefore didn't recognize Him around me, nor did I see the work He was doing on my behalf. My perspective was as an immature Christian who thought God was working only if I saw flashing neon signs showing exactly what He was doing and what I wanted Him to do. Well, as one of my favorite commercials puts it so eloquently: That is not how this works. That is not how ANY of this works. God doesn't have to or need to take direction from me. As a matter of fact, I am flat out elated that He doesn't—because I cannot pinpoint the number of times I would have settled for much less than what Christ has given in my life. I would have completely messed things up if I had been given control of my own life, because there have been many things, large and small, that I thought I wanted or needed that God has not allowed into my life. I've often failed to understand why—why God wouldn't honor my requests, my prayers. Sometimes I've been fine; I've accepted things as they were and moved on. But other times I've felt hurt, downtrodden, bummed, devastated, or, being completely honest, aggravated. Yes, I said it. I've been aggravated with God. That's not spiritual, you might say. Yeah, I know. But it's truth, and looking at the truths in my life has helped me WAY MORE than any of the pretending I have ever done!

The truth is that ALWAYS, no matter what—sometimes sooner, sometimes later—God has ALWAYS done what's best for me, and many times He has allowed me to see why His direction was best. He has even allowed me to see where He has saved me from very harmful, dreadful situations and places in my life. On the flip side, God has also blessed me by answering prayers in ways I didn't even know I wanted. Yes, Preston's accident was one of those ways, but there have been so many more. If we had time to just sit and talk about God's hand in my life, it would definitely take more than one or even two glasses of sweet tea. Here's just one example.

In 2006, when I was working at the local middle school, loving my job and getting a grasp on life again, God was very clear to me in His instruction that He would have me go to work at one of the local high schools. Well, I wasn't looking for another job, I hadn't applied for another job, and I didn't intend to change jobs, but God had different plans. Over the course of a few weeks, I continually felt God impressing on me to check the job register for our county teaching jobs. After trying to ignore the nudging, I relented. I checked the register. To my surprise, there was nothing. There were no teaching jobs for which I was certified, and I was relieved. Whew. I felt I'd dodged a bullet.

I'd like to say that that was the end of that, but it wasn't. A few days after finding that there were no jobs available, I felt God nudging me to check the register again. So, thinking there'd be nothing and that it would be an easy way to obey and move on (keep in mind that this was after Preston's accident, and I was learning to walk a new way), I checked the register as I'd felt led to do. This time, there was a position for which I was certified. Now, I would love to tell you that I immediately felt the leading of the Lord, and that I applied for the job with eagerness and anticipation, but that was not the case. For a few days, I just kept telling myself I was mixed up, and that God wasn't leading me to apply for the job. God couldn't want me to change jobs. I was so happy in the school I was in, and I felt like I was making a difference for my middle school students. I decided in my head that I was NOT going to apply for another job. There was no need.

HA! Yes, I find it funny now too. God wasn't *asking* me; He was *telling* me. And He kept telling me for several days, until one morning, as I was driving to work, I finally said out loud, while I was in the car by myself: "Okay, God. If you want me to apply for that job, I will. I don't understand it, but I will." I applied that same day, got a call for an interview a few days later, and was offered the job shortly after the interview. Now, get this: I distinctly remember telling the principal that I didn't want the job, and that I was going to have to think about the offer! To this day I can't believe she was so kind and understanding with me. She simply told me to think on it and give her a call back.

Well, God would not leave me alone until I said yes, and I praise His Holy Name that He gave me the gift I had no idea I wanted or needed. WHAT A BLESSING! I was able to work at the high school level for eight years and feed into the lives of those young people in ways I never knew God would allow me to. God taught me and grew me daily through my students. After I had gone through the storm of Preston's accident and being consumed for years with my own life and hardships, God put me in a position to give focus only to others. He placed me in situations within that school that allowed me to travel with my students, spend days on end with them year round, and become a part of their lives—not just their teacher. Placing me in that school, in that specific position at that time, was God's way of stretching me to focus on others and their lives, not my own. I still had plenty of storms and trials during these years. But God was teaching me how I didn't need to be consumed by them or drained by them. He knew how to move me to a new level of worship and walk with Him; a new level of reliance on Him. He just did it in a way I'd never dreamed of. Oh, how my heart was blessed during those years! Those students and faculty members became a part of my family. Many of those young people are my friends to this day, and there is no way I can fully convey the blessings and joy that I gained from a professional move I didn't want and was reluctant to accept. But God. God is always in control.

Another life lesson that I'm still learning is to simply take it all in; to **breathe life in**. Unfortunately, God had to make me stop to catch my breath. But after I remembered how to breathe in deeply and exhale deeply as well, I remembered what it was like to live fully. If our organs don't get enough oxygen, their functioning is hindered. Our spirits require the same thing—the breath of life. Preston and I have been learning not to skip anything, good or bad. We now try to be intentional in looking at all of our circumstances, without blinders. We try to see the details in what we perceive as good and what we perceive as bad. If there is any lesson I have learned in life, it is that things are not always as they seem. It's not healthy, nor is it our right, to look at, give time to, or acknowledge things, people, or circumstances that are pleasing only to us. God's spirit within us allows us to see things differently. We have the power to live differently. Preston and I are still learning to **count it all a joy**: The situations that appear unpleasing or difficult to us are situations where God can help us see His work and His will. Too many times, I have raced past opportunities to change someone's life because I didn't see the significance in what I could do; I didn't see where God could use me, or I didn't see God in the situation at all. I was acting like I was being chased by a wild animal or running toward a Reese's Peanut Butter Cup and a sweet tea! I was taking quick, shallow breaths that left me lightheaded and dazed. All I could see was the destination I was headed for or the catapult that had launched me to run. I could see good or bad but nothing in between—nothing in transformation or in progress.

Slowing down and taking it all in allows me to feel alive. It helps me find purpose. Slowing down to view the in-between gives me the chance to see the hand of God, the heart of God, the character of God. When I'm taking life in, I am taking the Holy Spirit deeper within me. Preston and I are still learning to make a conscious effort to see what God would have us learn or how He would have us be obedient to Him. Sometimes this involves sacrifice or serving or both. But opening our eyes to God's hands and truly seeking joy in all things reaps immeasurable blessings. God is all around us, moment by moment. It's up to us to breathe in His presence.

Now, please hear me clearly when I say that none of these truisms is automatic—knowing God is always in control, slowing down, breathing in all parts of life. We think there are people who have it all together, who are the ultimate Christians, who are so godly, but THERE ARE NONE PERFECT. That is scripture. That is truth. I am in no way floating through my life and my Christian walk flawlessly; not even close! Neither is that person(s) you envision as having it all together. We are ALL sinners, saved by God's abundant mercy and grace. No matter who you are, how long you've been a Christian, or when you accepted Christ, walking daily in the truths God has shared with us in His word will not be automatic. Serving God, searching to know God more, trusting God, looking for God, and praising God are all activities that require a conscious effort on our part. We are flesh. That is the purpose of the cross, Christ's death, and Christ's resurrection: WE NEED CHRIST MINUTE BY MINUTE.

Accepting Christ as your Savior doesn't mean you automatically become sinless. It doesn't even mean that you immediately make Him Lord of your life and seek Him in all things. Accepting Christ is the first step in growing Christ-like. We are all a work in progress. Once we reach our final form, God will call us to Heaven. That is truth. So please don't get bent out of shape when, after you've accepted Christ into your heart and proclaimed you are a Christian, you mess up, you sin, you act like you did yesterday. That is NOT what God sees! He is NOT keeping score! He is not surprised, because we are flesh. God realizes that it is a daily decision, a daily effort on our part to walk in His steps and turn from ourselves and our sinful ways.

What God does expect is that your heart wants forgiveness from Him. So ask Him. He delivers. Can we do whatever we want and then simply ask for forgiveness afterwards? NO. Not even close. But just know that it's okay if you're still working on trusting or on slowing down or on having faith or on whatever you struggle with. As Romans 5:3-4 states: "Not only so, but we also glory in our sufferings, because we know that suffering produces perseverance; perseverance, character; and character, hope." Keep on keeping on. Relax and enjoy life. It makes you stronger, and time is fleeting. You *are* moving forward as you build a character like Christ's.

Another lesson I've learned over the last several years is that **ALL of the Bible is TRUTH.** As humans, we are flooded with propaganda and marketing that tries to persuade us, influence us, and alter us. Unfortunately, we've taken that same practice into our schools, homes, and churches. Our beliefs have become so skewed and scrambled that, dare I say, many times we don't even know what we believe and why. Lines have become so altered in our lives that we know neither the foundations of our beliefs nor whether or not our beliefs are based on truth. As humans, we have become such followers that we find it too difficult to think outside of what the world around us would have us believe. We've grown so accustomed to this fast-paced, have-it-your-way world that we can't fathom the thought of researching the roots of why we do what we do. Nor do we take the time to learn new ways of operating.

This mindset has led most people to hold true to only parts of God's word. As a people, we have picked apart the Bible and recalled only the portions that satisfy us or serve our needs. I am NOT saying that we shouldn't learn memory verses, or that certain parts of the Bible aren't easier to recall than others. I am NOT saying that we must know and be able to quote every scripture in order to consider ourselves children of God. I am NOT saying that people who are more familiar with the Bible are better Christians, or that they are loved more by God. I'm simply acknowledging that, since I have been making a concerted effort to read God's word, dig in to God's word, and learn the message of God's word, I have begun to see that I cannot simply choose to believe some parts of what God is telling me but not other parts of what God is telling me. I cannot believe that God loved me enough to send His only Son to die on the cross, yet disbelieve the idea that, in the midst of chaos and pain, God will never forsake me. I cannot believe that God is coming for me again one day, and yet disbelieve the notion that I will have to give an account for my sins. Just because I can't see how things will work out or I can't bear the thought of having to stand before God in all of my shame, I do NOT have the option to overlook truth.

Some people ask: "If God is supposed to be a loving God, why would He have us stand before Him in shame?" I compare it to times in my own journey of raising my boys. I can recall a couple of times (not many, I'm sure the boys will tell you!) when they had misbehaved in some way and I'd had to find out about it on my own. I was bound and determined to punish them. Yet, when they came to me, confessed what they had done, told me they were sorry, and asked me to forgive them, I found myself relinquishing them of all wrongdoing and forgiving them on the spot. You see, when my boys did come to me, I could see the honesty in their eyes and the pain in their hearts. I knew that their shame and their disappointment in themselves were punishment enough—that they had learned a lesson. And so it goes with our Lord. God is a loving god, and He does want oh so much for us. But the Bible holds all truths, and there are words and directions in His word that are painful for us. Call them growing pains. I'm learning more and more that following requires intention and focus. Following requires honesty, humility, and humbleness. As the old saying goes: "The truth hurts." But as scripture says: "The truth shall set you free."

—

Preston's accident has also taught us both to **respect not only others, but ourselves and each other as well.** Preston and I were both raised to be respectful of others, and I feel like we've always done a pretty good job of that. But in becoming a part of each other's lives at such young ages and going through the teenage years of finding our way, we had lost respect for one another. To be brutally honest, we took each other for granted, and we were trying to demand respect from one another without giving any.

Preston and I are very different people. Opposites do attract. He is an introvert, a realist, very reserved, a thinker, very neat, and it takes a while for him to warm up to people. I, on the other hand, am an extrovert, a dreamer, all in, go with the flow, not neat (HA HA HA), and I love to meet new people. During the difficult time in our marriage, we now see, we were trying to change one another. We were trying to change the other person to fit our needs and be what we thought they should be. The worst part of it was that we weren't even verbally communicating what we wanted or needed the other to change. I guess we were hoping the other would just figure it out!

I have not once said that Preston and I were flawless or all that brilliant. Again, PRAISE GOD that He saved us from ourselves and our path of destruction. It really is true that if you treat others as you want to be treated, you will get that same treatment in return. I am quite slow in learning life lessons, but I eventually did figure this one out in my own home. Preston and I were both equally guilty in this area, and it has been one of the biggest changes in our relationship since the accident. When Preston started learning certain skills all over again, as if he'd never known them, we chose to start all over again in many areas as a couple—and mutual respect was one of the pieces of our foundation. We have learned to accept more readily that each of us offers our own unique contributions to our relationship, and that the ways we are so different are not that big of a deal and definitely not worth quitting over. God continues to help us grow in this area. But we still have our moments when he thinks I should just know something he has planned to do even though he hasn't told me about it—or when I leave my clean laundry on the back of the couch for several days and select my attire in the living room.

Another thing we learned from and since Preston's accident is that **we must armor up daily**. Just as God is alive and well and the Holy Spirit is real and within us, Satan is real as well. John

10:10 tells us that Satan comes to steal, kill, and destroy. Yes, he does! Satan will try any and every avenue to get to us, distract us, and keep us from focusing on anything that is connected with Christ. Furthermore, the closer we get to God, the more Satan will attack us. If he tries one way and isn't successful, he will try another and another and another. Many times, he will attack in numerous ways at once so that we don't even have the strength to realize what he's up to and call it like it is—a cheap shot! Satan is not fair. Satan is not gentle. He comes full force, with every ounce of energy and attack he can gather. He will disguise himself as anything and anyone possible to get to us. Be very aware that Satan believes in God, too; that's the very reason he will not let up. Even Satan knows the power of our mighty Savior. That's why he doesn't want us to know that very power. So, as the Bible says in Ephesians 6:10-18, we have to put on the full armor of God. Not only is it important that we put the armor on daily, it's also critical that we not leave off any piece. I have discovered from experience that there is a reason and purpose for each piece of armor named in scripture. If we get too lax and comfortable in a certain area or forget to put protection over a part of our lives, we can be certain that we are leaving a wide open target for Satan.

These aren't the only lessons we've taken away from this storm in our lives. I could go on and on and on. But these few capture many other lessons within them. It is my prayer that, as you read this book—especially the lessons that have been so critical for Preston and me—you will take the time to reflect, talk to

God, and listen openly as God reveals to you all the ways our story resonates with your own story and what He would have you learn in your own walk.

So here's the last lesson I want to share. It's big. It's scary for some. But it is truth: **The Holy Spirit is real.** Romans 8:11 is very forthright in telling us that the Holy Spirit lives in us, and that the power of Christ is within us: "Do you not know that your bodies are temples of the Holy Spirit, who is in you, whom you have received from God? You are not your own." All scripture is written for a purpose, and all of it is the truth. Whether or not we are comfortable with all scripture is up to us. For many of us, even if we were raised in a church body and have heard many teachings in our Christian faith, this truth in particular is one that we have heard very little about. So it can be intimidating. It has been my personal experience that the Holy Spirit or Holy Ghost is not generally the focus of many sermons or teachings. Even though I remember early teachings of the Trinity (Father, Son, and Holy Ghost), I don't recall specific teachings explaining the third part of that Trinity. I don't remember any explanations of the Holy Ghost, how we can tune in to that spirit, or how it should be revered as a part of our worship and relationship with God. Even though I accepted Christ as my Savior when I was nine years old and I experienced the Holy Spirit even then, it wasn't until I was older that I began to recognize the Holy Spirit rising and stirring within me.

Over the years, I have allowed myself to become more in tune with listening intentionally as I hear the spirit whispering to me. I've learned that when I feel compelled to move or act regarding a situation, I'm being led by the Holy Spirit. I've learned that when I am overcome with the presence of God around me, I'm being led by the Holy Spirit. I've learned that when I have no explanation as to why I must do something or I will miss a blessing, I'm being led by the Holy Spirit. There is so much more to be said about the Holy Spirit of God, and so much more I must learn, but please know that the Spirit of the Lord brings comfort, peace, assurance, redemption, guidance, and freedom. The Holy Spirit has led me to innumerable blessings and has saved me from countless heartaches.

I would love to say that, since I have begun learning more about the Holy Spirit, I have listened to and obeyed each of its leadings. But it's not true. There have been times when I've known the Holy Spirit is leading me to do or not do something, yet I have ignored the Spirit and paid for my disobedience. Just as it is with every other aspect of our walk with God, this is an area we need to nurture and feed in order to grow.

One of the major changes that ranks right near the top of the ways our lives were transformed by Preston's accident didn't actually come to fruition until years after the event. Even though God had begun the work of this particular change in the moments immediately after the accident, I didn't succumb to His direction until late fall 2011. (Have I mentioned that I am slow to give in to God's leading?)

What exactly was this big change? It was the call into ministry. I remember it quite vividly. It was post-accident, and I was attending my first-ever women's conference with some ladies at our church. I was hearing Beth Moore speak for the first time. As I entered the venue and looked at the sea of other women who had come to hear from and worship God, something washed over me: an overwhelming, stopped-me-in-my-tracks rush of heaven. It was in those moments when I heard God whisper to me that this was the purpose for which I was created. The presence of God was upon me so strongly that I could not move. I sat down in my seat, hung my head down, and cried from the depths of my heart—a cry so deep that it was one of the most intimate times of worship I have ever experienced. I had heard God, and I was coming to the realization that I was re-evaluating my life's purpose. I couldn't move. I don't know how long I just sat there, quiet and still.

Maybe you're sitting there saying to yourself: "So this chick thinks that God told her to be like Beth Moore?" Well, let me put your mind at ease. The answer is simple: No. Did I hear God say that He would give me a ministry known around the world? No. Did I hear God say that I would be an eloquent scholar of His word who can teach like no other? No. Did I hear God say that I was created to share His word and share the truth with all who will listen? YES! Absolutely, YES! God was clear in His direction to me: I was to speak to others and teach others. I had finally learned of God's real and true and abundant love and favor and grace and mercy, and that God had created me with the heart for others and the personality and ability to speak to others. He was directly telling me what I was to do with what He had given me.

Here's the part where I show my flesh: I did not give in to the call at that time. Even though I shared with a couple of ladies there that I knew God was calling me into ministry for Him, I made no movement to make it happen. I talked with God more regularly about what I had heard Him say, and I did accept that I'd been told by God that I should be in ministry, but I made no effort on my end.

Just as I had heard God whisper to me, I also began hearing more from Satan about the ministry idea. Remember: I had battled self-esteem and lack of self-worth issues since an early age. Well, Satan LOVES to attack me in those areas every chance he gets—and that's what he did. He began saying to me that no one would want to hear from me. He began asking me questions: "Do you really think God would speak through you?" "Are you forgetting the things you've done in your past?" "Are you aware that people won't listen to you because they know you and your sinful nature?" Satan was full of negativity. He came out swinging and continually delivered fast, hard hits to my mind.

I listened to these lies for a few years and tried to turn my calling into many other things. I sang in the praise band at church. It was great, and I really enjoyed it, but I knew it wasn't my ultimate calling. I participated in other areas of ministry one after the other, but I could never get God to change His mind and let me pick what I wanted to do—to take on a role I would be comfortable with. The more I tried to make something else be the way I was to serve, the more God made His vision for me clearer and clearer. As a matter of fact, I remember distinctly when God told me the exact name I was to give the ministry He would begin. This isn't glamorous, but it's the truth.

I was lying on the floor of my living room, eating a bowl of cereal. It was around 2006 or 2007, and all the guys were out of the house. It was very rare in those years for me to ever have the house to myself, but on this particular night I did—and I was choosing to eat my cereal in the living room. As I was eating, I began to think of Christ. I began to praise Him and thank Him for all He had done in my life; not just through the accident, but for all the days of my life. As I was praising and thanking God for who He is and how He had poured His love on me, He once again spoke extremely clearly to me. It was then that He named His ministry—the ministry I had not yet given into or formally begun: Blessed Beyond Measure. Later, as I began to put hands and feet to the ministry and officially began walking in God's call, the ministry simply took on the name of Blessed Beyond Ministries.

Now, the formal beginning of the ministry is yet another part of the story. As I had done many times, I was attending a women's conference. This particular one was at a local church, and I was excited to worship, praise, and fellowship with other ladies so close to home. Let me just go ahead and put this out there. Here again, you may not like my honesty, but I do hope you can appreciate the reasoning behind it. Someone needs to know this.

When I went to the conference that day, I was still trying to get other things to take the place of the call God had for my life. I thought that attending this conference locally was close enough to me being in ministry. I would be with women around the area, we could feed into one another's lives, and I'd be able to serve by sharing with other women. I went to this conference expecting to fulfill something for that day. Get that. It's so important. I went that day expecting to fulfill something for THAT DAY. I didn't go expecting or looking for ways to change lives from that day on. And I especially didn't go expecting or looking for my own life to change from that day on. I just thought I would take part in the conference, have a great day with God, and move on to the next thing.

Oh, how I was ever so wrong. I went into that church thinking I would do my part and go home. I came out knowing my part was about to begin, and that it would look like whatever God would choose it to look like, not whatever *I* would choose it to look like!

Here's how it went. We had finished the first session. We had taken a break and were worshiping through song before the speaker was to come in for the next session. As I began to worship, I felt that familiar stirring of God in my heart that was beginning to whisper to me again about how I was called to do speaking ministry/women's ministry. Well, of course, what did I do? I hung on to the pew in front of me for dear life. Truth be known, I think I was actually shaking that pew with a death grip, hoping God would let me just listen to what He had to say and move on. HA! That didn't happen.

All of a sudden, one of the musicians or the speaker announced that we were going to take one more quick break before the speaker would begin. CRAP! I didn't want the music to stop, and I most certainly didn't want any down time! I was afraid of what God might do next. And guess what? He did it!

As I stood there holding tight to that pew, God said: "Go and tell that lady that you are to be in women's ministry." Well, my first reaction as I was standing among hundreds of women was: "What lady, God? I am with lots of ladies." I thought to myself quickly: "Oh, God doesn't want me to do anything, because if He did He would be more specific. He wouldn't just tell me to go tell 'that lady.'"

As quickly as I could, I dashed out of the sanctuary and headed to a chocolate fountain that the church had set up as one of the many wonderful offerings of this conference. As I walked toward the fountain, I just knew God would see that I was busy and forget all about talking to me. I thought I would be able to avoid hearing God—to outrun him. The whole time I was walking toward the fountain, God kept saying again: "Go and tell that lady that you're supposed to be doing women's ministry." As I approached the fountain, I could see a doorway that led to what I thought was the room where book sales were taking place for the guest speaker. I was walking, and God was telling me to go and tell, but He didn't wait for me to ask for clarification this time—because He continued by saying that the lady I was to speak to would be right inside the doorway I was facing.

It was then that I surprised myself by not even stopping at the chocolate fountain. Instead, I walked right past it and into the doorway I felt so drawn to. Immediately inside was a table where a young lady was standing. The room was completely full of tables with young women standing at them, and there were many ladies walking throughout the room. Only by God's design and instruction did the next steps unfold. God completely orchestrated every moment that followed. I walked up to the lady at the first table in the room, and as quickly as I could I spit out these words: "Hello, I am Karen Solise, and I don't know why I'm supposed to tell you, but God told me to come and tell you that I'm supposed to be in women's ministry." I didn't take a single breath during this entire sentence, and I'm pretty sure I stated it in record time. I was just so relieved to have gotten the words out of my mouth that I could have jumped over the table that stood between us at that point. There is no doubt in my mind that I could have jumped over that table from a flat-footed position! To say that I felt instant relief is an understatement.

But here's what blew my mind: The young lady to whom I had just issued this life-changing proclamation gave me the sweetest smile and answered in such a gentle and kind voice. She said: "Hello, I'm Shelly Johns, and I'm from the Baptist Women's Association. How do you feel about speaking? Speaking in front of others?" I smiled and gave a little chuckle before responding: "I'm a teacher. Does that count? I feel like speaking is exactly what God is calling me to do." Shelly and I talked for a bit. She told me more about herself and the BWA, then asked if I would be interested in hearing more about being put on the speaker list for the organization. She gave me her card, and we then parted ways.

Obeying God and sharing with Shelly that day brought me a peace that is unfathomable to our human minds. A peace like what I experienced that day is received in our spirits and then allowed to be transferred to our minds.

After that encounter with Shelly, I began to pray and seek God's guidance regarding the beginning of a ministry. But this time, I took things further and put my hands and feet into action. Within a couple of months, all things were in order and God and I embarked on a new journey: Blessed Beyond Ministries. Since then, God has opened doors I could never have imagined. I've had numerous opportunities to share the word of the Lord through speaking engagements and ministry events. God has allowed me to serve Him through serving others, and He is continuing to grow His ministry for His glory.

It is yet another blessing that has come from Preston's accident. I know; that sounds weird and farfetched, right? Well, I agree with you to an extent, but let's look at it this way: Had the accident not occurred, I may not have had another opportunity to snap out of it, get it together, or smell the coffee! Had I not come to the realization that my life was quickly spiraling into just an existence, I may never have truly experienced the love of Christ—the immeasurable, merciful, gracious, all-knowing, selfless love of Christ. If I had not experienced God's love the way I had, I would not have anything to tell. There would be no need for me to be in ministry. I would not have been able to share something I didn't have, nor could I have spoken of and described something I hadn't experienced myself.

God is in control of all things. This ministry, which God has led me to, has allowed me to speak freedom to others. I have experienced that freedom. This ministry allows me to share how God has changed my life, our lives—how He saved me, how He loves each of us and He desires each of us. I have experienced

His redeeming salvation and love, and I know of His desire for me. Sometimes I share my testimony. Other times I do not. Scripture and Biblical truths are the foundation of this ministry that God continues to allow me to be a part of.

Let me be clear: It's not only I who gives to this ministry; it requires a family effort. Preston is more than supportive. He encourages me and helps in every way possible to allow me the time I need. Both he and my boys sacrifice attention I would give them so that I can serve others. And God leads, even though my initial reaction to His call was not one of excitement or anticipation.

I am truly blessed beyond measure.

8

*I*f you're wondering about our lives today, I don't even know where to begin. Our boys are now twenty-five and twenty-two, respectively, one a recent college graduate and the other scheduled to graduate next year. They are beautiful young men, and they are my heartbeat.

Preston and I strive to embrace every aspect of life and to live completely reliant upon Christ. God is still sustaining us as Preston and I continue seeking to walk in His steps. We are FAR from perfect. If you're looking for that, look to Jesus. We fail to serve God the way we should in every situation, our witness to others is not what it should be one hundred percent of the time, we still bicker from time to time, and we still get caught in our old selves every once in a while. But one thing I can say without hesitation is that our lives have changed for the better. Granted, our lives continue to be far from calm, typical, and routine. Not only does Preston still deal with the pain and limitations that resulted from the 2004 accident; he now suffers as well from another injury that occurred in 2013, while he was working underground—an injury that ended his mining career. He's had one neck surgery and is facing more, all the while unsuccessfully seeking approval for disability. Even though he has been denied for disability four times, we hold tight to God's promises, and we continue to see God's hand upon us. Preston is unable to work, or do much of anything, due to the pain and limitations of his body. BUT GOD is at work, and Preston continues to count it all a joy. He witnesses with his story, and he continues to say that he wouldn't take back any of what has happened to him. When asked if he ever wants to question God with "why me?" his response is always a quick "why not?"

While writing this book has been therapeutic, it has also brought out demons and darkness. It has been difficult for me to deal with the memories, the emotions, the stress, the perceptions, the rawness, and the feeling of being exposed. For the last several months as this process has unfolded, Satan has been coming at me full force. I have been surrounded by the storm all over again. Putting myself back into the mindset of the person I was before has regurgitated thoughts, feelings, and insecurities that have fought for my peace. I have surrounded myself with the hurts and the flesh aspects of that trial. Writing my story has opened a door to my past to a time when I was not surrounding myself with Christ-like tools (like scripture and godly thought processes). I have found myself going back to pull information, yet actually being back in my old self, my old mindset.

I have felt the oppression of Satan throughout this process of writing, telling me I'm not enough and that no one wants to hear our story. He has told me repeatedly that my words can't possibly help anyone. He has attacked me in my personal life, my professional life, and, more than anything, in my very own mind. He uses me against me. BUT GOD. In writing this story I have put myself out there; raw and vulnerable. Yet as I experience these feelings and fight these attacks, I know I'm not alone. Oh, I know now that I wasn't alone last time, but I didn't know it then; I didn't claim victory in Christ. Now, though, because I know that God's word is truth and that He is all He says he is, I've found myself running after Him as fast and as hard as I can. I have found myself crying out to Him, seeking Him at every turn.

Ultimately, my goal in this book is to help others see Christ and be assured of His great love, forgiveness, mercy, and grace. Writing it has been yet another spiritual marker for me. The process has been a cleansing, reflective self-assessment that has been teaching me more about me, my relationship with Christ, and the untainted character of God. It has taken me into a deeper reliance on Christ, a closer walk with Him. I have found myself searching out His word, seeking scripture of direction and guidance. I've sat quietly and utterly still to hear God and what He would have me say and share. And in the end, I have been completely unharnessed and honest about myself in my flesh, my flaws, and my mistakes.

Completing this book has gotten me to a point where I have to face the reality that some people may take offense to my honesty, while others will be distanced from me because of my flaws and my blatant openness about them. Isn't it ironic that God would choose to use someone like me—someone who had always clung to the thought that my performance was all that defined and represented me—and have me write (perform) as He speaks to me? He has made it a point to show me that this is not MY performance, but HIS; I must rely on Him. I have nothing to say without Him.

My deepest desire is that you hear God in every word of this book; that you see Him in every aspect of this story; that you feel His presence with you, and that you soak the Holy Spirit of God into the depths of your being as you read. Whether you're on a mountaintop or in the lowest valley you 've experienced in this life, I'm praying continuously that reading these words will bring you a renewed spirit, a new freedom, a deeper acceptance of God's favor for your life. Maybe you've been saved for years because you asked Christ to be your personal Savior a long time ago. Maybe you're a new Christian and have recently accepted Christ. Or maybe you've never met Jesus. Wherever you are, my prayer—and my ultimate purpose in writing—is that you gain a deeper understanding of the character of God and His unfathomable love for you personally, as well as His deep desire to bless you.

God wants to remove us from the quicksand and the sinking pit in which we place ourselves. But He can't lift us if we don't extend our arms to Him. If reading these words has prompted you to learn anything about Christ, then my heart's desire has been met. But as I said previously: I began this process for you, but I'm feeling quite selfish as I come to a close because of what this process has done for me. I have learned many things, but one major thing is that NOTHING is impossible with God. He will use my obedience. I just have to keep trusting and obeying. I find it ironic that "Trust and Obey" is one of my favorite hymns from childhood. The songwriter was correct: There is no other way to be happy in Jesus than to trust and obey. You see, when you pray, God listens and always answers. Sometimes we get a "yes." Sometimes we get a "no." Sometimes we get a "maybe later." The scriptural truth we can cling to is that God's answer is for our best. So if God doesn't answer your prayers quite the way you'd like Him to, maybe it's because He has something better for you.

My walks around the little track near my hometown helped me experience the power of prayer on an entirely new level. It was from these walks and talks with Jesus that I learned that PRAYER CHANGES THINGS, and I began to get a glimpse of the power of my prayers. Know this, absorb this, let this sink to the depths of your soul: Your prayers have power. Your prayers might bring safety. Your prayers might bring clarity. Your prayers might lead to salvation for a soul. Or your prayers might do for you or someone else what my prayers began to do at that track all those years ago: Your prayers might save someone from mere existence and set them on the path to truly living.

Even though I wasn't in the mine with Preston on April 10, 2004, there is no doubt in our hearts, minds, and souls: It was prayer that brought Preston and I out of the darkness and into God's light. Remember that the night is darkest before the dawn. No matter how circumstances appear, God's light is all powerful and He is in control. Your morning—your light—is coming.

ACKNOWLEDGMENTS

Clayton and Tanner Solise—for making me a momma and bringing such joy to my life.

Momma and Daddy (Janet and Larry Dame)—for giving endless support, for being the hardest-working people I know, for teaching me and giving me a solid foundation in life, and for being such *awesome* people.

Tamara and Tom Dever and the TLC Graphics staff—for believing in me and obeying God's call on their lives.

Thank you, God, for walking with me step by step.

ABOUT THE AUTHOR

A Kentucky girl, born and raised, Karen has been married to her high school sweetheart, Preston, for nearly 30 years. Together they have two sons, now 23 and 26. Karen has been in education for 19+ years and has served in ministry in multiple ways over the last 25 years. She is the founder and president of Blessed Beyond Ministries and LOVES sharing God's word and what He has done in her life. Karen's deepest desire is to reflect Christ in such a way that it directs others straight to His grace, mercy, love, and freedom.

Christianity doesn't make everything
perfect, but with God—
and a glass of sweet ice tea—
an imperfect life can be full of joy.

Showing others how to find joy in God's presence is her passion.

Life is so sweet if you just let it be.